Midterm Campaigning and the Modern Presidency

Midterm Campaigning and the Modern Presidency

Reshaping the President's Relationship with Congress

Michael A. Julius

 PRAEGER™

An Imprint of ABC-CLIO, LLC

Santa Barbara, California • Denver, Colorado

Library of Congress Cataloging-in-Publication Data

Names: Julius, Michael A., author.
Title: Midterm campaigning and the modern presidency : reshaping the president's relationship with Congress / Michael A. Julius.
Description: Santa Barbara, California : Praeger, 2018. | Includes bibliographical references and index.
Identifiers: LCCN 2018008307 (print) | LCCN 2018023053 (ebook) | ISBN 9781440845178 (ebook) | ISBN 9781440845161 (hardcopy : alk. paper)
Subjects: LCSH: Executive-legislative relations—United States. | United States. Congress—Elections. | Political campaigns—United States.
Classification: LCC JK585 (ebook) | LCC JK585 .J85 2018 (print) | DDC 324.7/20973—dc23
LC record available at https://lccn.loc.gov/2018008307

ISBN: 978-1-4408-4516-1 (print)
         978-1-4408-4517-8 (ebook)

22 21 20 19 18   1 2 3 4 5

This book is also available as an eBook.

Praeger
An Imprint of ABC-CLIO, LLC

ABC-CLIO, LLC
130 Cremona Drive, P.O. Box 1911
Santa Barbara, California 93116-1911
www.abc-clio.com

This book is printed on acid-free paper ∞

Manufactured in the United States of America

Contents

Acknowledgments

Although the genesis of this book was the product of a rare moment of intellectual clarity on my own part, a project of this scale is always the work of many hands. As an extension of my graduate dissertation, I would be remiss not to thank the instructors and students of the University of Minnesota—most especially Drs. Liz Beaumont, Timothy Johnson, Kathryn Pearson, and Joe Soss—for aiding me with and guiding me through a mountain of work of which this book represents merely the visible peak, and it would not have been possible without a wide range of data, most importantly the congressional and presidential data sets of Dr. George C. Edwards III and Dr. Gary Jacobson. For its transition to book, I need to extend my thanks to Jessica Gribble, my favorite editor in the world, without whose assistance, prompting, and (most importantly) patience, this project never would have been finished. Finally, to my wife, Lindsay, my sincere thanks for allowing me all the time I needed to work on this and for never reminding me too stridently of my promises that it would be done "this week."

CHAPTER ONE

The Place of Midterm Campaigning in American Politics

The office of the president of the United States is an inherently dangerous one. Lacking the restraint required of a prime minister by the necessity of retaining a parliamentary majority, or of the collegial veto used in analogous ancient institutions, the American president possesses political independence; great institutional resources; a long, fixed term; and a limited and convoluted method of removal. Moreover, any given president, presuming he has policy goals, has every incentive to push against and bend the rules, to subvert existing norms, and to try to move as much political power to the center and to himself. Not without reason did many Anti-Federalists argue that the presidency would be little more than an elective king and that it was an institution too dangerous to allow in American society.[1]

Though the modern presidency—even at its most impressive—hardly matches the fever dreams of presidential domination foretold by Anti-Federalists such as "Cato" and Patrick Henry during the debates over ratification, the 2016 cycle certainly proves the problematic status of the presidency in American politics.[2] I do not mean that the cycle or the ultimate election of Donald Trump was somehow intrinsically bad, but rather that it made clear that the presidency has pushed aside or completely demolished most of the traditional restraints that held it in place. Though this transformation can be seen in any number of ways, you can see this most clearly with one of the most important restraints, the party system.

For both major parties, the 2016 presidential cycle laid bare the simple fact that the candidates control the party, not the party the candidates. The

Democrats saw their nomination process hijacked and nearly derailed by an individual who is declaredly not a Democrat, and the Republicans saw a deep and talented field mowed through by a man who, in the past twenty years, has been a Republican, an independent, a third-party member, and a born-again Republican—all while donating heavily to major Democratic figures, including his eventual opponent.[3] Yet neither party could effectually gain control of its own nominating process (and the Democratic party suffered potentially mortal losses by having the gall to try to do so).[4] The presidency—as an office and as an idea—has fully subordinated the party to itself.

The subordination of the parties has coincided with the transformation of the presidency from a constitutional office into a popular one. It may on paper mirror the pseudo-elected monarchy of the Roman consulship, but in practice it more closely resembles the later tribunate—an office imbued not with legal power, but popular authority, whose purpose is to defend the people against the power of the state and of the elites.[5] Presidents have transformed their office from one built on formal authority (*imperium*) to one built on informal power (*auctoritas*), and now rest their strength on the popular will.[6]

There are many potential reasons that could be offered for the dominant position of the presidency in American political life. Blame could be apportioned to voter apathy or ignorance, and special approbation given to TV and the internet for allowing us to both be distracted by the trivial and poisoned by the insidious.[7] It could be argued that the American polity never really recovered from the crisis of confidence it felt due to Vietnam and Watergate, and that scandals (real and imagined), shutdowns, and policy failures have led the public to become disillusioned with government. Any number of reasons could be offered for the current state of affairs, but the purpose of this book is to add one more—a powerful and misunderstood tool of the modern presidency: presidential midterm campaigning.

Conventional Wisdom

The academic conception of the modern presidency is fairly well encapsulated by two statements by the quintessential scholar of the modern presidency, Richard Neustadt. The central thesis of *Presidential Power*—that presidential power is the power to persuade—serves as the foundation for the entire conception of the modern public presidency. But *Presidential Power* does more than claim that the presidency *can* persuade, but rather asserts that it *must* persuade, and that any unilateral action—no matter how constitutional—represents a failure.[8] Woodrow Wilson famously argued in *Constitutional Government* that "the President is at liberty, both in law and conscience, to be as big a man as he can"; Neustadt famously appended a coda: "But nowadays he cannot be as small as he might like."[9] This notion that a modern president is fundamentally different from his predecessors defines the logic of the "modern" presidency—both as a feature of government and an object of study. Moreover, it suggests a level of finality to the matter. It is as if, like Caesar, the nation had at some point come to a moment of terrible significance and that—*alia jacta est*—the presidency and the nation have crossed some political Rubicon.

In so defining the study—and really the nature—of the modern presidency, Neustadt's fundamental arguments also shaped and shape the study of any area of presidential behavior that gets classified as "modern." This includes the study of presidential midterm campaigning. This makes sense: the behavior did not manifest in a sustained way until after the Second World War and appears similar to other facets of the modern presidency (such as the permanent campaign). Unfortunately, this emphasis on modernity, and hence on Neustadtian formulations, has caused problems for the study of presidential midterm campaigning.[10]

For one, Neustadtian ideas of persuasion and "obligation" have shaped the basic assumptions of this behavior. If presidential power is ultimately about persuasion; if much of that persuasive power is focused on Congress; and if persuasion is more easily exercised by presidents over co-partisans than over others, then it follows that presidents ought to use midterm campaigning to boost the chances of their fellow elephants or donkeys in midterm races. The occasional heretical thinker will venture to think that presidents are not so other-regarding, and that midterm campaigning is priming future presidential voters to support the right candidate during the re-election, but it is still about presidential persuasion. Consequently, the study of midterm campaigning takes as its foundational concept the idea that the behavior is about presidents persuading voters to take particular actions in the voting booth.

While this is a logical assumption to make and fits with overall conceptions of the modern office, I would suggest it has led to a poor understanding of the presidential involvement in congressional campaigns. Having assumed a "why," research moved on to the logical method of testing—looking at whether presidentially supported candidates did, in fact, win their elections (or at least do better). Finding that they did not, the study of midterm campaigning languished, with early work (such as Campbell, 1980) largely being left alone until fairly recently.[11] Because presidential campaigning did not produce the (statistically significant) results demanded by research, the research on this topic largely vanished, and when it came back (such as Herrnson et al., 2011), it largely kept the same assumptions and got the same results.[12]

This suggests a problem for the study of this behavior. Either (1) presidents are spending a king's ransom in resources on a behavior that has literally no measurable impact on congressional elections and therefore no return on investment, or (2) we are starting from the wrong assumptions, thus asking the wrong questions and getting the wrong answers. Why might we be wrong?

Problems

The first problem with the traditional understanding of midterm campaigning is that it is too insistent on the Neustadtian notion of the distinctly modern presidency. This sets up a straw man argument within the literature, in which a "modern" presidency is contrasted against its "premodern" equivalent, as if there were a switch that changed the office from one to the other. This furthers not only the false conception that the modern presidency is purposefully different, but also that the earlier presidency represented a sort of stunted, adolescent phase of the office. As Steven Skowronek notes in *The Politics Presidents Make*, although Neustadt does many valuable things, the idea of the "modern" presidency, "the notion of a prior age when presidents did not have to be leaders . . . is nothing more than a conceit of modern times."[13]

This creates two interconnected problems in our conception of the midterm campaigning and the modern presidency that obstruct both the progress of knowledge and our conceptual understanding of American politics. First, the idea that the contemporary presidency is motivated by a different set of passions or interests than its antecedent forms is a dangerous result of misplaced nostalgia and overt self-importance. The "modern" presidency is certainly distinct from "premodern" presidency in terms of its means—*how it acts*—but there is little reason to suspect it is any different in terms of its ends—*why it acts*. Jefferson hoped to control the political environment no less than did Obama; that the desire made itself manifest in different ways does not make it less true. Thus, conceptions of the modern presidency and of the way it behaves frequently make this distinction, to their detriment.

Second, in addition to supposing that the behaviors of the "modern" presidency, particularly midterm campaigning, are motivated by distinctly modern concerns, scholarship on midterm campaigning also presumes that the behavior has something of an obligatory character to it. Because presidents can campaign, they do campaign, and because they do campaign, they must campaign (and must campaign to the advantage of their co-partisans). This conception not only denies the presidency any agency in its undertakings, but it ignores (or denies) the basic fact that midterm campaigning as it is done represents the choice of a certain course of action over others; a decision to invest limited recourses in one way rather than another.

By thus boxing in our understanding of the behavior, these assumptions obscure potential paths of investigation and understanding. To begin with, by suggesting that presidential involvement in (midterm) congressional elections is little more than the logical extension of the modern, public presidency, we obscure any possibility of any other rationale behind the activity; we make no progress in really understanding "why" the behavior occurs. Indeed, we do not need a "why"—the behavior exists because it must. This is an incredibly problematic condition, as it causes us to effectively ignore a wide range of potential motivations for a behavior that consumes a huge amount of presidential time and energy during every midterm cycle, some of which could point to a profoundly different purpose for, and impact of, said behavior.

Likewise, the operative presumption that midterm campaigning is largely about either presidential or congressional electoral needs further narrows our range of vision with regard to this behavior and effectively leaves us with a potential "how," "where," or "who" of two—presidents must focus on either states that are important in a subsequent election or on congressional races that need assistance. This suggests that presidents are not, in fact, individuals motivated by policy, but rather by a scorecard. Why else would we presume that all they care about is the electoral outcome and not the subsequent (and far more substantively important) legal and policy outcomes that occur as a result of elections?

Finally, seeing the behavior as predestined and obligatory obscures its potential impact and importance. This is because what the behavior can do is, to an extent, a function of why it is done—at least, if it is done thoughtfully and well. Consequently, by simply advancing the thesis that midterm campaigning is merely another unexceptional facet of the modern presidency and that it happens to the combination of the vicissitudes of fate and the whims of others, we lose sight of what midterm campaigning might actually be accomplishing—because we are looking in all the wrong places.

Different Foundation and Different Questions

To assess midterm campaigning in a new light, it is necessary to lay a new foundation. Rather than grounding its assumptions in the Neustadtian modern presidency, this book grounds itself in presidency presented by Steven Skowronek. As he adeptly put it in *The Politics Presidents Make*, the presidency is

> an office that regularly reaches beyond itself to assert control over others, one whose deep-seated impulse to reorder things routinely jolts order and routine elsewhere, one whose normal activities and operations alter system boundaries and recast political possibilities.[14]

This disruptiveness is a necessary by-product of the place of the presidency within American politics—the office most imbued with public "trust," but lacking in the constitutional means to effectively carry it out. As Woodrow Wilson pointed out over a century ago concerning the limitations of the presidency, "the constitutional structure of the government has hampered and limited his action [with regard to leadership], but it has not prevented it."[15] Presidents have the potential to create political change, but they lack the internal means to achieve it and are hampered by the nature of the constitutional order. As a result of this, presidents must constantly seek to reorder the political universe if they are to be successful, to find ways to strengthen a surprisingly weak hand. Unsurprisingly, scholarship is replete with presidential efforts to reshuffle the deck, from attempts at executive mastery of the bureaucracy, leveraging of presidential tools in interbranch bargaining, or even illegitimate constitutional aggrandizement.[16]

Midterm campaigning has disruptive potential just as great as any of these, as the behavior hits at three of the major restraints on presidential powers. For one, it has the ability to influence the relationship between the president and the voting public (in a manner distinct from the simple "public presidency"), and more broadly, it has the ability to influence the relationship between the president and the electoral resources needed to secure (re)election. Although "campaigning" may—in the personal, in-front-of-the-public, pressing-the-flesh sense—be seen as less important today than it once was, it allows the president the capacity to directly interact with the public in a manner far more substantial than all the televised speeches in the world can. Thus, by giving the president a ready-made reason to reach out to the public in a visceral sense, midterm campaigning effectively supplies the president an additional bite at the persuasion apple in years two and six. Consequently, it potentially allows the president not only the capacity to shape immediate electoral outcomes but also the opportunity to attempt to reshape the political environment and dispersion of political resources in years four and eight— and beyond.

Likewise, midterm campaigning can (obviously) influence the composition of Congress. These are, after all, congressional elections alone, and the victors will help or hinder a president for the following two or six years. If, as most scholarship contends, the purpose of midterm campaigning is what it appears to be—the election of more partisans to office—then successful midterm campaigning can alter the balance of power in Congress and the governing capacity of the president and his allies. Presuming that the president possesses policy ambitions, this is a most desirable thing, as congressional assistance is needed for most any long-lasting goals. Thus, the behavior can remove one of the primary constitutional obstacles to presidential ambitions.

Finally, midterm campaigning also impacts the makeup and nature of the American party system. If the behavior can impact voters and Congress, then the ways it can impact parties should be obvious. Beyond this, midterm actions can also impact the parties by putting the weight of the president behind certain factions within the party. If the Freedom Caucus were wiped out on the Republican side, or the Blue Dogs on the Democratic, you would see major changes in the behavior of that party, changes that would either help or hinder a president's agenda. If midterm campaigning has substantive value for candidates—if it carries weight with voters—then it could also work the other way, and midterm campaigning could help presidents to "prune" their party in the way they wish, advancing certain streams of thought and restraining others.[17]

Seeing midterm campaigning in this light, as a potentially disruptive force to a trio of major restraints on presidential actions, suggests a very different way of viewing the behavior and very different questions that need to be asked to understand it.

1.   *What is this behavior disrupting?*

Public presidential participation in congressional elections—midterm or otherwise—is a relatively new phenomenon, and one which has not always been accepted by the political order. The Founding Fathers were against it, and premodern attempts to engage in it did not go well for presidents.[18] Thus, we need to understand what the relationship between the presidency and Congress was "intended" to be, and in what way was this relationship and the political system established to support it subverted by presidential campaigning. Likewise, we need to understand how the political order (i.e., Congress) reacted to early attempts at presidential involvement, how they perceived their place, and what has changed to allow congressional acquiescence.

2.   *Why do presidents engage in midterm campaigning?*

If we take it for granted that midterm campaigning is not merely the requisite outcome of modernity or something presidents merely have to do because they are partisans, then it must instead be seen as a conscious choice on the part of presidents—a conscious choice to change their behavior, to break with tradition, to attack an established way of doing things. Midterm campaigning does not occur, and did not come about, in a vacuum, but represents a set of actions chosen at the expense of other options. Presidents could have maintained the forms of the 19th century, throwing the weight of their office behind certain individuals and operating out of public view; engaging in public campaigning forecloses this option and is not without costs. Therefore, we need to understand what motivated and motivates this decision, what factors aid or hinder it, and why the behavior has developed as it has over time.

3.   *Why do presidents campaign the way that they do?*

Presidents want to achieve some set of goals in midterm campaigns, and they have limited resources with which to undertake them. Consequently, there must be some level of strategy and choice that animates their actions and their direction of resources. The way this is approached is invariably a function of the prior question, as whatever motivates presidents to engage in this behavior will shape their strategy. But either way, we must understand why presidents campaign where, for whom, in what fashion, and as frequently as they do. Midterm campaigning is not inherently straightforward, and each president undertakes it in a different manner. Does this suggest they want the same thing or something different, and how can we tell?

4. *What do presidents get in return for their actions?*

Much ink has been spilled looking at the impact of campaigning on electoral returns, and the victory or defeat of given candidates. However, we need to move beyond this simple dyadic question of whether the candidates that presidents aid win or lose; there could be so much more going on that we lose out on by having such a narrow gaze. If midterm campaigning is so unsuccessful at altering election results, then why is it done? What does it do in the election cycle itself, or in the future, that has sufficient value to presidents to justify the investment of resources? Moreover, how does this fit with the first two questions above—does midterm campaigning represent a conscious strategy or an obligatory response to basic political pressure?

Different Tools

To look at midterm campaigning in a new way requires not only new questions but also new tools. One of the biggest weaknesses of existing scholarship is that it focuses on states or races rather than candidates, suggesting that the people who make up a given party are themselves interchangeable, and that what matters are the dynamics of the race rather than who they happen to be. In particular, this overlooks the importance of the relationships that exist between political figures—ironic, if the power of the presidency is the power to persuade.

Thus, if we are to better understand the place of midterm campaigning in American politics, we need to be able to understand how presidents relate to and interact with the candidates on whose behalf they invest so much time and effort. Existing scholarship is largely focused on these behaviors in the aggregate or as interchangeable actions on the individual level—that is, it is not the candidate who matters per se, but the dynamics of the particular race. However, this ignores the simple fact that the power of the presidency is the power to persuade, then we have to understand the relational aspects of this behavior if we are to properly understand why president campaign, whom they campaign for, and what they get in return.

To this end, I have created the Midterm Campaign Database, a compendium of every event held, candidate interacted with, and public statement made by presidents in the course of midterm campaigns from 1954–2010. These data (described in greater detail in Appendix A) allow the examination of midterm campaigning with a greatly increased level of detail, as it is possible to parse not only between those whom presidents campaign for and those they do not, but also in how they campaign for them and even how they speak about them (an example of this can be seen in Chapter 5). This should make it far easier to see the difference in the relationships that presidents have with given sets of candidates, as those differences will be far more nuanced.

Plan of the Book

With this in mind, the book advances so as to both lay a foundation for and sufficiently answer each of these four overarching questions. This begins in Chapter 2, with the theoretical framework of the book, which is based on a conception of the "intended" relationship between the political branches of the federal government, itself rooted in the Madison aversion to "parchment barriers." It argues that the separation of powers system of the American Constitution was built to improve on the Whig Settlement of 1688 through a series of formal and informal restraints to presidential action. It shows that 19th- and early 20th-century reforms to these constitutional restraints served to ensure that new barriers would be erected to presidential dominance each time the old ones were torn down; these changes certainly acted to increase presidential capacity over time, but they also ensured that the fundamental purpose of the constitutional settlement would be retained. The chapter closes by arguing that midterm campaigning represents a break with this pattern and an activity that undermines the intended balance.

Chapter 3 explores this framework by looking at the "premodern" attempts at midterm campaigning, undertaken by Andrew Johnson (1866), William Howard Taft (1910), and Franklin Roosevelt (1938), and the reactions to them by Congress. It argues that in these cases the political order acted as "intended"—presidents acted to upend the political and/or partisan order of their day, and in the face of these presidential attempts, Congress and the party system reacted by attempting to enforce presidential compliance by impeaching (in the case of Johnson) or ostracizing (for Taft and FDR) the president. Moreover, it argues that these cases show that we cannot understand midterm campaigning merely through the lens of the modern or public presidency—that status existed at least by 1938, if not by 1910, and it certainly was of no comfort to either Taft or FDR. Thus, whatever "allowed" midterm campaigning by subsequent presidents was not a lack of technical or physical ability to undertake the campaigning—or even a lack of public acceptance—but rather an aversion within both Congress and the party system to presidential meddling.

If this is the case, then it raises the question of what changed in the political order to give presidents such free reign for their actions; this question is dealt with in Chapter 4, which argues that rather than reflecting a new presidential tendency—the desire to master both Congress and their party—the adoption of midterm campaigning reflects the collapse of the institutional ability of other actors—both in Congress and in the party system as a whole—to restrain presidential behavior. Particularly drawing on the transformation of the party system over the 20th century, the chapter shows that the weakening of these restraints has freed presidents to engage in midterm campaigning as they see fit, transforming the behavior from one ostensibly designed to aid their fellow partisans to one deliberately practiced to aggrandize the presidency. It closes with an empirical examination of the growth of the behavior, showing how the partisan realignment of the later 20th century fueled the explosion of midterm campaigning.

To show how this change plays out in the world of practical campaigning, Chapter 5 examines how this changed behavior plays out in the campaign season, by looking at presidential campaign strategy. Specifically, it looks at the *who, when, where*, and *how* of midterm campaigning. Contra existing work, this section shows that presidents do not focus their efforts on aiding vulnerable co-partisans or on merely trying to maximize their party's share of House and Senate seats, but rather that they deliberately structure their endeavors to reshape Congress—and, specifically, their party in Congress—in their own political image, even if that risks seats in marginal districts or states.

The results of this presidentially driven strategy are examined in Chapter 6, which explores the impact of midterm campaigning on the subsequent election as well as the future behaviors of both Congress and the electorate. It shows that rather than being an inconsequential behavior on a practical level—the frequently found failure to influence election returns—midterm campaigning has important impacts on congressional voting behavior and on the shape of the future electorate. Put together, it finds that midterm campaigning reshapes the composition of both the party in the electorate and the party in government, moving both into positions more favorable to the political inclinations of the campaigning president.

In the concluding chapter, I step back to take a wider view of the place and importance of presidential midterm campaigning in the American political order. If midterm campaigning happens for the reasons, in the manner, and with the impact that is described in the three preceding chapters, it suggests some fairly significant outcomes for general American politics, not all of them "good." The chapter examines these in their own light and in the ways they fit with the "constitutional design" laid out in Chapter 2, paying particular attention to the potential impacts of disconnects between the two.

Notes

1. Moreover, many Anti-Federalists argued it was an institution that only came into being due to the actions of the Committee of Style sneaking in changes at the end of the convention. See, for example, "Genuine Information," by Luther

Martin, in Herbert Storing, ed., *The Complete Anti-Federalist*, Vol. 2 (Chicago: University of Chicago Press, 1981).

2. See, for example, the "Letters of Cato" or Patrick Henry's speeches to the Virginia Ratifying Convention (particularly those of June 4 and 5) in Herbert Storing, ed., *The Complete Anti-Federalist*, Vols. 3 and 5 (Chicago: University of Chicago Press, 1981).

3. According to the *Washington Post*, Donald Trump changed his party registration five different times between 1987 and 2017. Jessica Chasmar, "Donald Trump Changed Political Parties at Least Five Times: Report," *Washington Post*, June 16, 2015, https://www.washingtontimes.com/news/2015/jun/16/donald -trump-changed-political-parties-at-least-fi/.

4. This is the animating argument of Hillary Clinton's retrospective on the 2016 election. Hillary Clinton, *What Happened* (New York: Simon and Schuster, 2017).

5. The *Tribuni Plebis* were magistrates elected solely by the lower order in the Roman political system (the plebeians), to protect them against the actions of the senatorial class. The tribunes could veto the enactment of laws and stop the actions of senatorial magistrates against a plebeian, and were held to be sacrosanct during office. See Livy's *Ab Urbe Condita*, II, 33, for a discussion of the birth of the office. This concept was in the mind of the Founding Fathers, as Governor Morris discussed the merits of having the president fill this role in American society during the debates of the Constitutional Convention. Max Farrand, ed., *The Records of the Federal Convention* (New Haven: Yale University Press, 1911, 1937), Vol. 1, 511–14 (July 2, 1787).

6. *Imperium* and *auctoritas* are archaic terms from Roman legal thought, but nevertheless I think they best represent the argument that I am trying to make here. They represent the two sides of the coin of power: *imperium* expressed the power held within and through a legally constituted office, and *auctoritas* represented power that was held through some form of personal claim on affection, trust, or leadership from the body politic. Cicero, for example, held (in *De Legibus*) that the makeup of the Roman political order was *potestas* ([basic physical or political] power) with the people, *imperium* (formal or constitutional/legal authority) with the elected magistrates, and *auctoritas* (informal/moral authority) with the Senate. As an example of this, when a magistrate was elected, there was always an interregnum between the election and when the given individual was installed in office; during the interregnum, this individual was held by the Senate to have *auctoritas* and therefore to receive some measure of deference, even though he lacked the *imperium* that would be held following his formal installation. Relatedly, Caesar Augustus claimed (in his *Res Gestae*) that he held power within the Roman world not through some level of actual political power (*imperium*), but rather because, of all actors, he had the most *auctoritas*—the people desired that he should lead. *Imperium*, then, is a widely studied topic: indeed, all of constitutional scholarship and theory is devoted to it (though perhaps unknowingly). *Auctoritas*, on the other hand, rarely enters the literature.

7. Numerous authors have made this argument, such as Markus Prior, *Post-Broadcast Democracy* (New York: Cambridge University Press, 2007).

8. Richard E. Neustadt, *Presidential Power and the Modern Presidents* (New York: The Free Press, 1990)—hereafter *Presidential Power.* Neustadt discusses these instances in Chapter 2 (Three Cases of Command).

9. Woodrow Wilson, *Constitutional Government in the United States* (New York: Columbia University Press, 1908), p. 70—hereafter *Constitutional Government;* Neustadt, *Presidential Power,* p. 6.

10. The arguments advanced in this book are, on one level, merely about presidential campaigning on behalf of congressional candidates and are equally applicable to non-midterm campaigns. The work focuses on midterm campaigning because those cycles allow a unique window on presidential action, as they are midterm election and not presidential elections as well. Therefore, in studying midterm campaigning (rather than all campaigning on behalf of congressional candidates), we do not have to worry about attempting to parse out which campaign actions are done to benefit the presidential campaign and which are done to benefit those running for the House or Senate. Isolating the elections provides the opportunity, therefore, for greater clarity on intent, action, and result.

11. A number of scholarly works came to this conclusion, such as James E. Campbell, "Explaining Presidential Losses in Midterm Congressional Elections," *Journal of Politics* 47, no. 4 (1985): 1140–57.

12. Paul Herrnson, Morris Irwin, and William McTague, "The Impact of Presidential Campaigning for Congress on Presidential Support in the U.S. House of Representatives," *Legislative Studies Quarterly* 36, no. 1 (2011): 99–122.

13. Steven Skowronek, *The Politics Presidents Make: Leadership from John Adams to Bill Clinton* (Cambridge, MA: Cambridge University Press, 1997), p. 5.

14. Ibid., p. 4.

15. Wilson, *Constitutional Government,* p. 57.

16. Marissa Martino Golden, "Exit, Voice, Loyalty, and Neglect: Bureaucratic Responses to Presidential Control during the Reagan Administration," *Journal of Public Administration Research and Theory* 2, no. 1 (1992): 29–62; Joseph Cooper and William West, "Presidential Power and Republican Government: The Theory and Practice of OMB Review of Agency Rules," *Journal of Politics* 50, no. 4 (1998): 864–95; William G. Howell and David E. Lewis, "Agencies by Presidential Design," *Journal of Politics* 64, no. 4 (2002): 1095–114; Cameron, Charles Cameron, *Veto Bargaining: Presidents and the Politics of Negative Power* (New York: Cambridge University Press, 2000); Louis G. Fisher, *Presidential War Power* (Lawrence, KS: University of Kansas Press, 2004); William J. Quirk, *Courts and the Congress: America's Unwritten Constitution* (New Brunswick, NJ: Transaction Publishers, 2008); Francis Wormuth and Edwin Brown Firmage, *To Chain the Dog of War: The War Power of Congress in History and Law* (Urbana-Champaign, IL: University of Illinois Press, 1986).

17. President Trump has hinted at a desire to do this with the Freedom Caucus of the Republican Party.

18. Much has previously been written about the fear of demagoguery at the time of the Founding. Indeed, this is part of the focus of the very first of the Federalist Papers. But though the Founders were concerned about presidential speech, they also felt that it would likely be judged as less important than speech made by speakers with local attachments—such as members of Congress; "premodern" attempts at midterm campaigning are discussed in Chapter 3.

CHAPTER TWO

Sketching the Relationship between the President and Congress

The Constitution of the United States is an exercise in structure, not substance; it creates a framework for the American government, but it does not tell that government how to act. Far from being the "Newtonian" machine described and vilified by many in the 20th century, the authors of the document understood that the problems of self-governance could not be solved on pieces of paper.[1] Thus, it does not, as Madison cautioned, put its faith in "parchment barriers," but relies instead on the ambition and passion of real actors.[2] This is particularly true of the balance of power between the Congress and the presidency. Rather than being rigidly defined in the text, it is structured by a series of factors—both textual and extra- or a-constitutional—that shape the incentives and motivations of the political actors and thus structure their relationship.[3] How those relationships evolve has profound implications for American politics.

Presidential involvement in congressional elections—midterm and otherwise—is both an influence on and a symptom of the changing relationship between the president and the Congress. To understand the importance of this behavior in our political development, we need to look at how it changes the relationship between the president and Congress, and how that ripples through the broader political system. This can be difficult, as it is risky declaring that the dynamics of the American constitutional order are "x." The presidency may be more powerful and the Congress more quiescent, but more powerful and more quiescent than what? The problem with any study of American political development is that it must make assumptions about what the political order was (or was intended to be) in order to argue how it has changed. This is made particularly tricky by the fact that, on paper, the formal constitutional order of the United States has changed very little—at least in terms of how the federal government is structured and operates internally.

The purpose of this chapter is to make an argument for what the framers of the Constitution intended the relationship between the president and Congress to be, to serve as a theoretical framework for the remainder of the text. To this end it connects the Founders to the then long-standing Whig Settlement[4] and shows how the Constitution sought to improve upon it by better insulating the Congress from executive meddling. It then shows how changes to the political order in the 19th century—namely the creation of the party system—increased the possibilities of presidential power but also took steps to better restrain it. Finally, the chapter looks at the 'reforms' of the early 20th century, namely the rise of the rhetorical, public presidency. Although this certainly did transform the presidency, it did so in a way that did not inherently threaten the existing political order; the same cannot be said for presidential involvement in (midterm) congressional campaigning.

Sketching an Original Design

It would be foolish to claim that I *know* what the authors of the American Constitution intended, or even that they intended any specific outcome or set of outcomes.[5] This is not to say that the document is devoid of meaning or open to an interpretation, but rather an acknowledgment that the document is more the product of compromise than any discrete theory of government, and its final form driven more by the Committee of Style (and the desire to go home) than by the body as a whole.[6] Moreover, our best contemporary exegesis of the Constitution comes in the form of the *Federalist Papers*, our reverence for which causes us to generally overlook both the competing understandings of the Anti-Federalists (some of who attended the Philadelphia convention), and the fact that the essays of Publius were written to win votes, not to be truthful.[7] As we can neither positively identify the "author" of the document, nor the process of its creation, it is doubtful we can authoritatively declare its meaning in any reasonable fashion.

Thus, rather than trying to divine the intent of the document, it seems the best way to examine the desires of the Founders is to step back from an attempt to understand what they wrote and instead focus on the major political beliefs and motivations that we can easily identify as being shared by the framers of the Constitution. I want to focus on two of them specifically. First, the men who assembled in Philadelphia in the spring and summer of 1787 were, in broad strokes, Whigs.[8] Indeed, one way to understand the American Revolution is as a continuation of the English Civil War—a domestic struggle between

American Whigs and Tories, with the Whigs triumphing (and the Tories moving to Canada).[9] Thus, the elites of the newly independent United States had a shared set of political beliefs that traced back more than a century to the struggles between Parliament and the King in the English Civil Wars and Parliament's ultimate triumph over the House of Stuart in the Glorious Revolution of 1688. This meant that, although they also drew on Continental (Montesquieu) and Scottish Enlightenment thought (Hume), they overwhelmingly drew from the philosopher of the Revolution, John Locke.[10]

Claiming them as (to a man) post–Glorious Revolution Whigs is not to suggest that the framers of the Constitution were of the same mind on every topic—one need only look at Hamilton's suggestion of an elected monarch to see that[11]—but rather that they were committed to a shared set of underlying principles. Namely, they shared with their political kinsman of a century prior the idea that in any government the legislative power must predominate and that the executive must be closely watched. This belief ran so deep that "to proponents of the Whig school of thought, representation is only possible in a numerous and locally elected legislative body."[12] The government of the Articles of Confederation as well as many of the early state governments reflected this tendency, with strong legislature and weak (or nonexistent) executives.[13] This was a function of an underlying fear of arbitrary power—an empowered legislature is inherently less efficient than an empowered executive, but the friction that slows down the chamber also ensures that a broader set of voices will be heard.[14]

The political system that came into being from this pure Whig school of thought underpinned a second political motivation widely shared by the Philadelphia delegates, a belief that the existing political structure—made up of strong legislatures and weak (or nonexistent) executives—was not conducive to the long-term health of the United States.[15] The inability of the Congress to uphold its own laws under the Articles of Confederation,[16] among other tribulations, made it clear that some form of capable executive was needed if the general government was to be successful. Madison, in particular, "sought to find ways to enhance both the independence and authority of [the presidency]."[17] This raised concerns for many American elites—particularly the Anti-Federalists—who saw arbitrary power and despotism as the certain result of a powerful executive.[18] So deeply ingrained was this fear that it is doubtful that a capable executive could have been established had it not been for the presence of Washington at the convention, his willingness to serve in the office, and the ample number of times he had shown an aversion to dictatorial powers.[19]

The trick for those assembled in Philadelphia was to find a way to ensure that the legislature would predominate while also investing the presidency with sufficient powers as to be effective and useful for the new government. "Congress was regarded as the central political institution, but what was also provided for was the strongest possible executive under the circumstances."[20] This attempted balance was, of course, at the heart of the Hamiltonian defense of the presidency in *Federalist* nos. 67–77. These essays are our best window into the role of the presidency envisioned by the authors of the Constitution,[21] and they served as an extended argument as to why a powerful and competent executive is not dangerous to liberty—or, as he put it in *Federalist* No. 70, "Energy in the executive is a leading character of good government."[22] The trick for the delegates in Philadelphia was to find a way to create this energetic executive in such a way that they could also convince the ever-watchful Anti-Federalists that the presidency did not pose a threat. One way that they were able to do this was by going back into their ancestral political history and shamelessly copying the core of the Whig Settlement of 1688, the English Bill of Rights, the acceptance of which was the price of William of Orange's (and to a lesser extent his wife, Mary's) crown.

This is obvious in the fact that the Constitution of the United States heavily cribs its century-old antecedent. This was done for good reason, as the goal of the English Bill of Rights was to ensure that the issues that had occurred between King and Parliament did not continue to re-emerge and that the monarchy could exist alongside a predominant legislature; it was for all intents a guidebook on achieving the goals of the Federalists. To ensure the predominance of Parliament while maintaining the beneficial aspects of the monarchy, the English Bill of Rights pledged Parliament's allegiance to the sovereigns while also laying out a set of specific restrictions on the power of the monarch(y). For example, the fourth provision that William and Mary pledged to uphold was "that levying money for or to the use of the Crown by pretense of prerogative, without grant of Parliament, for longer time or in other manner than the same is or shall be granted, is illegal."[23] This is echoed in Art. II, § 8.1 and 9.7, which gives the sole power of taxing and borrowing to Congress, and requires that all monies spent by the federal government be explicitly authorized by Congress. By giving Congress the power of the purse, the Constitution ensures that Congress authorizes any major action of the presidency—at least obliquely. Thus, a nation can have a capable executive alongside a predominant legislature.

Likewise, a fundamental fear held by the Whigs of 1688 was that the monarch could use his control over the military to oppress both parliament and the public—much like they believed both James II and his father Charles I had attempted to do. To this end, the Bill of Rights requires the King to acknowledge "that the raising or keeping of a standing army in the kingdom in time of peace, unless it be with the consent of Parliament, is against the law."[24] This restraint on executive control of the military is echoed in Art. II, § 8.12–16, which gives Congress control over raising, regulating, and paying the military. Neither sought to eviscerate executive control over the military: the president remains commander in chief, and the monarch remains the titular head of the British military. Rather, both the English Bill of Rights and the American Constitution sought to restrain these powers through legislative oversight and legislative predominance.

But American founders were not merely slavish imitators of their forbear-ers. Rather than merely plagiarizing the prose of their antecedents, they made use of the experiences of the intervening century to improve upon the Whig Settlement in important ways. One way they did this was by refashioning the relationship between the legislature and the executive envisioned by the prior constitutional order. This was because the British system of King, Lords, and Commons had emerged out of the continental idea of the three estates. From its beginnings as an advisory and tax-approving body, the British Parliament (the estates of the Lords and Commons) eventually gained the sole capacity to make law—or at least the acceptance that law could not be made without its acquiescence.[25] This meant, however, that the monarch retained sole exec-utive authority. This was a true separation of powers, but also an inherently unstable environment.

This constitutional settlement was unstable because it contained within it the possibility of the very absolute and arbitrary power that the Whigs feared. This was because by suggesting that all legislative power was held by the Parlia-ment and that the sovereign held all executive power, the constitutional order that came out of the Glorious Revolution allowed for the possibility of unilat-eral action by the king and unilateral (institutional) action by the Parliament. The fear of arbitrary power, though perhaps more palpable in the executive, was still present in a government controlled through the legislative branch; as Jefferson famously noted, "History has informed us that bodies of men, as well as individuals, are susceptible to the spirit of tyranny."[26] To combat this possi-bility of dominance by the legislature, each branch of the federal government is constituted separately but given powers that effectively require assistance from another branch to carry them out. As Richard Neustadt famously observed, "The Constitutional Convention of 1787 is supposed to have created a govern-ment of 'separated powers.' It did nothing of the sort. Rather, it created a government of separated institutions sharing powers."[27]

The Founders likewise deviated from their Whiggish ancestors in tackling one of the most glaring weaknesses of the political order established follow-ing the Glorious Revolution. Whereas the English Bill of Rights required that parliamentary elections be free and frequent, and that the king not interfere in the internal debates of Parliament, it did not instruct the king not to inter-fere in those free and frequent elections.[28] This proved a huge impediment to the true implementation of legislative predominance in Britain, as the sover-eign possessed a number of tools with which he or she could easily manipu-late the makeup of Parliament, effectively supplanting the legislature as the dominant power. By elevating individuals to peerage (something rarely declined), the monarch could both stack the House of Lords in order to secure favorable outcomes in that chamber while correspondingly pulling recalcitrant members of the Commons out of the chamber and therefore altering vote counts in favorable ways.[29] The king or queen could distribute patronage in the form of ministerial positions as well as jobs reaching back into the depths of British history that carried with them sizable salaries or pensions. And if all else failed, the sovereign could use their own resources to directly interfere in elections.[30] Consequently, even though the Parliament was predominate, the king or queen in Parliament, through their ministry, could frequently dictate electoral and therefore political outcomes.

The American Constitution restrains the presidency's capacity to so interfere and thus helps to better preserve legislative predominance. Presidents are denied the ability of directly interfering in the composition of the Senate by requiring that it be chosen by the state (legislature or voters) or by the state's governor; they do not get to treat the Senate like a House of Lords.[31] Presidents cannot entice members of the Congress with ministerial portfolios in exchange for ongoing support, as members of the House and Senate are forbidden from simultaneously holding a position within the executive branch.[32] Finally, presidents cannot (or could not, historically) easily interfere in elections as they lacked independent resources within their office: they had no presidential estates from which to draw the necessary funds and could not (legally) make use of public funds for such a purpose.[33] Thus, by a more adroit mix of combination and separation, the American founders better insulated Congress from executive interference.

Nineteenth-Century "Amendments"

Although the founding design did improve on the Whig Settlement, it soon became apparent that this solution came with problems of its own. True, by divvying up the powers of government and giving sufficient independence to each branch that "ambition might combat ambition" they succeeded in making it harder for the constitutional order to be overthrown, but they also made it significantly harder for governmental power to be used at all.[34] By creating this system of "separated institutions sharing power," the Constitution increased the difficulty of both tyrannical and legitimate action.

Madison made clear in the *Federalist Papers* that we are neither angels, nor can we expect angels to come and govern us.[35] Yet, for the original Madisonian system to function, it effectively required angelic individuals—persons of goodwill, elected from across a large and diverse space, who nevertheless shared the same general preferences and possessed a willingness to compromise in the name of the public good. It required that American elites share a common worldview. However, it became clear early on in Washington's administration—particularly after the return of the Jay Treaty to the United States—that there were fundamental differences in how American elites saw the world.[36] These differences very quickly led to the organization of Hamilton's Federalists and Jefferson's Democratic-Republicans. Although some scholars are fond of arguing that the Constitution is ready-made for and designed in anticipation of a party system, the emergence of party system in the late 18th century is largely accidental—though certainly inevitable.[37]

Parties are far from angelic, but they do offer a solution to the lack of unifying tendencies within the constitutional structure. By establishing different electoral methods and different electoral bodies for the House, Senate, and presidency, the Constitution successfully insolated the Congress from executive interference; it also succeeded in isolating members of the legislature from one another. The election of members from individual states and districts— by different voters and at different times—meant that the Congress was (and is) inherently parochial, and focused on local rather than national considerations.[38] This is problematic in a nation as large and diverse as the United States, as the needs of various areas are going to wildly differ from one another, and loyalties would as likely be to the periphery as to the center.[39]

Parties offered a way past this problem, through the notion of "parties in government." By connecting "the personal relationship and provincial loyalties formed in localities and states with the national government," parties can bridge the isolation brought on by the constitutional order and ensure real democratic participation in government.[40] Thus, "the party system helped ameliorate republican government's greatest vulnerability—public indifference."[41] As such, parties were tools that allowed greater and more effective collective action by animating both the public and the elites, and by organizing them into more cohesive units.[42]

However, each change in efficiency creates a corresponding change in the likelihood of tyranny. By bridging the geographic divides between members of Congress, and the institutional divides between the House, Senate, and presidency, the party system made it easier for the government to get things done. But it also removed some of the separation built into the original Constitution and therefore some of the protection against presidential overreach. This was less of a problem during the hegemony of the Jeffersonian Democratic-Republicans, as the congressional caucus system of presidential selection worked to subordinate presidents to Congress. However, with the collapse of this system in the election of 1824 and the immense, demagogic yet unelected power of Andrew Jackson over the following four years, the dangers of the early party system were thrown into stark relief.[43]

A solution to this was the revitalized second party system, constructed largely by Martin Van Buren. Although the newly minted Democratic Party was initially a vehicle for Andrew Jackson's triumphant 1828 campaign for the White House, the efforts of Martin Van Buren and others helped to ensure it had not only long-term viability but also long-term value.[44] Van Buren and his allies deliberately constructed the party—and the soon-to-follow Whig party imitated them—with local power bases as a means of constraining executive power.[45] Presidents might at times be immensely powerful, but as a general rule they were merely *primum inter pares*—the first among equals—and they needed the assistance of state and local leaders if there were to accomplish anything.

Thus, although the institution of the party system altered the contours of the American constitutional order, it did not attempt to overthrow it. This was because whereas the party system did empower the president, it also empowered Congress by binding presidential success to the corresponding success of congressional partisans. Thus, it served to further tie presidential needs and ambitions to Congress rather than those of Congress to the president. By diffusing the power of the party apparatus to other actors and by tying presidential success to theirs, it constrained the threat of arbitrary power while increasing the functional capacity of the government. This allowed the advantage of a partisan system (greater opportunities for collective action) while not sacrificing the underlying Whig-inspired desire (restrain executive ambition).

Progressive Attacks

Although the party system did empower the presidency, it restrained it as well. This restraint—and the constitutional order in which it existed—came under attack by the Progressive movement in the early 20th century. Lodged in both parties, the Progressives were reformers who wanted to use the power of government to deal with problems emerging from the industrialization of the nation. One of the most important intellectual leaders of this attack was Woodrow Wilson. As a noted academic before entering politics, Wilson helped to literally determine how we speak—and therefore think—about the American government, and his intellectual enemy was the heart of the constitutional system implemented by the British and American Whigs: the presidency restrained by the separation of power. As Tulis points out, "For Wilson, separation of powers was the central defect of American politics. He was the first and most sophisticated proponent of the now conventional argument that 'separation of powers' is a synonym for 'checks and balances'—that is, the negation of power by one branch over another."[46]

To counter the actions of the Founders, Wilson promoted a consistent theme of reform, one that was also supported by his contemporaries: a push for "efficient government." Wilson was an acolyte of Walter Bagehot, the famous essayist, who believed that the American system was fundamentally flawed, as "at a quick crisis, the time when a sovereign power is most needed, you cannot *find* the supreme people."[47] Wilson seconded this by arguing this failure to be the result of the preeminence of the Constitution in American politics, noting that if in his day the English constitution had grown superior to the American, "it is so because its growth has not been hindered or destroyed by the too tight ligaments of a written fundamental law."[48]

In the name of efficiency, Wilson bent his mind to overcoming the separation of powers, and his touchstone was that *"power and strict accountability for its use* are the essential constituents of good government."[49] He believed that the problem with the political order was that these two principles were disrupted by the nature of the separation of powers. As Wilson remarked in *Constitutional Government*:

> The makers of the Constitution constructed the federal government upon a theory of checks and balances which was meant to limit the operation of each part and allow no single part or organ of it a dominating force; but no government can be successfully conducted upon so mechanical a theory. Leadership and control must be lodged somewhere.[50]

The solution to this was to spur the development of leadership within the public sphere. Leadership, to him, was not an abstract concept, but a vital source of purpose and energy for a nation. As he noted in *Leaders of Men* (1952):

> In what, then, does political leadership consist? It is leadership in conduct, and leadership in conduct must discern and strengthen the tendencies that make for development. The legislative leader must perceive the direction of the nation's permanent forces and must feel the speed for their application.[51]

For the American government to fulfill its purpose, a set of leaders had to emerge capable of bending the legislature to their will; only in this way would the national will be realized. Leaders were to be forceful; ruthlessly single-minded; ideologically driven; and, above all, partisan—"A party likes to be led by very absolute opinions: it chills it to hear admitted that there is some reason on the other side."[52]

Thus, to allow him to claim effective and legitimate leadership without recourse to constitution change, Wilson required that the president shake off the restraints of the Jacksonian system and become the leader of his party. His theory of politics "required that the president focus the public gaze on Congress to such an extent that individual legislators felt compelled to support his initiatives."[53] By the time he wrote *Constitutional Government*, Wilson already believed this to be an established fact. He thought this role was created by the nature of presidential selection and that the president "cannot escape being the leader of his party except by incapacity and lack of personal force, because he is at once the choice of the party and of the nation. He is the party nominee, and the only party nominee for whom the whole nation votes."[54]

The president as party leader would be able to bridge the divide between the branches and to bring about a more efficient government without the need for constitutional change—or rather, with "constitutional change" in lieu of changes to the Constitution.

These Progressive "reforms" represented a clear threat to the Whig order of legislative predominance in the constitutional order. The Jacksonian party system might have upset certain facets of that order, but it also acted to maintain them by tightly binding the ability of the president to succeed to the willingness of his party to support him. Wilson—and, importantly, his spiritual successor Franklin Roosevelt—thought that rhetorical presidency possessed the capacity to reverse the partisan relationship, binding the party to the president and thus effectively subverting congressional predominance. As Wilson famously put it, "If he leads the nation, his party can hardly resist him. His office is anything he has the sagacity and force to make it."[55]

But was he correct? Perhaps not. Wilson certainly discovered the limits of the rhetorical presidency in his push for the Versailles Treaty, and FDR in his question to pack the Supreme Court. In the end, rather than breaking the system of legislative predominance, the rhetorical presidency—on its own—merely highlights the strength of it. "Going public," for example, highlights rather than diminishes the constitutional structure that promotes congressional predominance. It can only be effective when either (1) a member of the president's party has strayed significantly from the wishes of their local electorate, or (2) a member of the opposition is cross-pressured by voters who are buying what the president is selling. It is a testament to the fact that American politics is still localized in many respects and that the president has remarkably few tools with which to bludgeon Congress directly; it shows the strength of the balance between the ideas of the legislative predominance and independent executive capacity, rather than its collapse.

What About Midterm Campaigning?

The American constitutional order is predicated on a balance between the desire for legislative predominance and the need for a capable executive to carry out the law. To square this circle, the Framers relied on a series of formal and informal conventions that limited presidential ability to interfere with the workings and composition of Congress. The Framers thus improved upon the traditional Whig constitution by helping to ameliorate one of the primary problems of the post–Glorious Revolution constitutional settlement—namely, the ability of the monarch to greatly influence the makeup of the Commons and Lords.

However, the American revisions worked all too well, and the constitutional structure was quickly amended in the early decades of American political history with the introduction of the party system. While this sought both to increase political participation and make it easier for elected officials to work together, it too acted to restrain the president just as it empowered him. By centering the party apparatus at the state and local level, and by requiring that the president gain and maintain the support of that apparatus to gain or stay in office, the 19th-century party system tried to allow greater cooperation between branches while still restricting presidential involvement in congressional affairs.

The early 20th century presented a major challenge to this order, in the form of "constitutional" reforms enacted by President Woodrow Wilson. Wilson attempted to graft a British style of parliamentary politics into the American separation of powers by establishing the president as a rhetorical and partisan leader—effectively attempting to establish a Westminster-style ministerial system within the United States. But even the corresponding rise of the rhetorical presidency did not upset the underlying political balance, as it largely left the political relationship between the Congress and the presidency unchanged. True, the president could now directly speak to the public, but to the extent his rhetoric had impact, it required the support of as-yet independent senators and representatives to be carried into effect.

Presidential involvement in congressional campaigns, however, presents a different kind of threat to the constitutional order. This is because although the rise of the party system and the rhetorical presidency were overt, public assaults on the then existing order, presidential involvement in congressional campaigns has the possibility of reworking the political system in a far more covert and subtle manner. In spreading power among institutions, the Constitution forces the branches to work together; it forces them to bargain.[56] Thus, as Neustadt correctly pointed out, the ultimate presidential power is the "power to persuade."[57] However, Neustadtian politics is overt, elite, and geographically bound; the president, in this case, negotiates with Congress and persuades fellow elites to take action. By hijacking public discourse, and by moving political discourse outside of Washington, involvement in congressional campaigns empowers one side without correspondingly aiding the other.

This is why midterm campaigning is so important. Involvement in congressional campaigns has the capacity to reshape the relationships that exist between actors—the possibilities of persuasion—in ways uniquely fruitful to presidents. By directly canvassing the voters, directly raising money, and potentially determining of their own accord for whom they will and will not campaign, such presidential involvement has the possibility to upend the specific notion of partisan restraint on presidential actions that has existed since the mid-19th century and the general notion of legislative predominance within the American polis.[58] Consequently, it ought not to have been received well, and it was not. The next chapter explores the ways that the political order reacted to midterm campaigning by premodern presidents and the ways in which the existing political order of each time asserted itself in the face of attack by the president.

Notes

1. Woodrow Wilson, *The New Freedom* (Garden City, NY: Doubleday, Page, 1921), p. 47; Alexander Hamilton, John Jay, and James Madison, "Federalist 48," in *The Federalist*, eds. George Carey and James McClellan (Indianapolis: Liberty Fund, 2001), p. 256.

2. Ryan J. Barilleaux, *The Post-Modern Presidency: The Office after Reagan* (New York: Praeger Press, 1988), p. 48.

3. Ibid., p. 147.

4. By Whig Settlement, I mean the political order that was established in England following the Glorious Revolution of 1688. For details on this topic, see, inter alia, *The Constitutional History of England Since the Accession of George III* (May) or, of course, the works of noted thinkers such as Blackstone for more detailed analyses of the subject.

5. A good examination of the varying methods of understanding the Constitution through the intention of the Framers can be found in Richard Loss, "Presidential Power: The Founders' Intention as a Problem of Knowledge," *Presidential Studies Quarterly* 9, no. 4 (1979): 379–86.

6. James Rakove and Susan Zlome, "James Madison and the Independent Executive," *Presidential Studies Quarterly* 17, no. 2 (1987): 293–300—hereafter "Independent Executive"; Luther Martin, *Genuine Information*, in Herbert Storing, ed., *The Complete Anti-Federalist*, Vol. 2 (Chicago: University of Chicago Press, 1981).

7. As one scholar aptly put it, "James Madison's compelling Federalist essays left the mistaken impression that the Constitution's final design matched his own ideas for American government, and that these ideas essentially shaped the document." David Brian Robertson, Madison's Opponents and Constitutional Design," *American Politics Review* 99, no. 2 (2005): 225, 243.

8. In using the term "Whig," I mean it in its British sense—the opponents of the "Tories" in the period running up the American Revolution. This is not to confuse them with the later "Whigs" who emerged in the 1830s, though the allusion was intentional, as the Whigs of Henry Clay desired to present themselves as having coalesced in opposition to "abuses" of King Andy in the same way that the Whigs of the 17th century formed in opposition to the actions of the House of Stuart.

9. Kevin Phillips, *The Cousins Wars: Religion, Politics, Civil War, and the Triumph of Anglo-America* (New York: Basic Books, 1999).

10. Thomas Pangle, "Executive Energy and Popular Spirit in Lockean Constitutionalism," *Presidential Studies Quarterly* 17, no. 2 (1987): 253–65—hereafter "Executive Energy."

11. Max Farrand, ed., *The Records of the Federal Convention*, vol. 1 (New Haven: Yale University Press, 1911, 1937), pp. 282–93.

12. Gary L. Gregg II, "Whiggism and Presidentialism: American Ambivalence toward Executive Power," in *The Presidency Then and Now*, ed. Phillip G. Henderson (New York: Rowman and Littlefield, 2000), p. 69—hereafter "Whiggism."

13. James McClellan, *Liberty, Order, and Justice: An Introduction to the Constitutional Principles of American Government* (Indianapolis: Liberty Fund, 2000), pp. 147–50—hereafter *Liberty, Order, and Justice*.

14. Frank R. Strong, Judicial Function in Constitutional Limitation of Governmental Power (Durham, NC: Carolina Academic Press, 1997), p. 9; see also John Locke, *The Second Treatise on Government*, Chapter X, for a discussion on the problematic nature of arbitrary power (for the Whigs).

15. McClellan, *Liberty, Order, and Justice*, pp. 242–46.

16. It should not be forgotten that it was the Congress of the United States that declared itself to be deficient and incapable of functioning effectively; it is a truly remarkable thing. As Tocqueville noted, "If ever America showed itself capable of rising for a few moments to that lofty renown which the proud imagination of its inhabitants would constantly wish to reveal to us, it is was at that moment of supreme crisis when the national authority had in some way abdicated its dominion." Alexis de Tocqueville, *Democracy in America*, translated by Gerald Bevan (New York: Penguin Classics, 2003), p. 132.

17. Rakove and Zlome, "Independent Executive," p. 295.

18. See, for example, Letters of Cato, November 8 and 22, in Herbert Storing, ed., *The Complete Anti-Federalist*, Vol. 3 (Chicago: University of Chicago Press, 1981).

19. This is a well-noted trope, but covered well in Forrest McDonald, "Presidential Character: The Example of George Washington," in *The Presidency Then and Now*, ed. Phillip G. Henderson (New York: Rowman and Littlefield, 2000).

20. Pangle, "Executive Energy," p. 282.

21. Though one could also consider the Pacificus and Helvidius Debates of the Washington administration to be equally instructive in how little the authors of the Constitution agreed on concerning the president's role. See Alexander Hamilton and James Madison, *The Pacificus-Helvidius Debates of 1793–1794*, ed. Morton Frisch (Indianapolis: Liberty Fund, 2007).

22. Alexander Hamilton, John Jay, and James Madison, "Federalist 70," in *The Federalist*, eds. George Carey and James McClellan (Indianapolis: Liberty Fund, 2001), pp. 362–69.

23. "English Bill of Rights," The Avalon Project, Yale Law School, http://avalon.law.yale.edu/17th_century/england.asp.

24. Ibid.

25. William B. Gwyn, *The Meaning of the Separation of Powers* (New Orleans: Tulane University Press, 1965), p. 26.

26. Thomas Jefferson, "A Summary View of the Rights of British America," The Avalon Project, Yale Law School, http://avalon.law.yale.edu/18th_century/jeffsumm.asp.

27. Neustadt, *Presidential Power*, p. 29.

28. "English Bill of Rights."

29. Thomas Erskine May, *The Constitutional History of England* (London: Longmans, Green, 1978), pp. 15–23.

30. Perhaps the most famous example of this was in the 1784 General Election, where William Pitt the Younger used the resources (at George III's behest) to secure a stable majority for his ministry.

31. U.S. Constitution Art. 1, § 3.

32. U.S. Constitution Art. 1, § 6.

33. As Art. 1, § 9 notes: "No Money shall be drawn from the Treasury, but in Consequence of Appropriations made by Law; and a regular Statement and Account of the Receipts and Expenditures of all public Money shall be published from time to time." Moreover, as Hamilton comments in Federalist No. 73, the Constitution restriction on altering the pay of the executive is, in part, designed to insulate American politics from dangers arising from erratic presidential resources.

34. Alexander Hamilton, John Jay, and James Madison, "Federalist 51," in *The Federalist*, ed. George Carey and James McClellan (Indianapolis: Liberty Fund, 2001), p. 268.

35. Ibid., pp. 267–72.

36. See, for example, John Aldrich, *Why Parties? A Second Look* (Chicago: University of Chicago Press, 2011), pp. 70–102.

37. David K. Nichols, "A Marriage Made in Philadelphia: The Constitution and the Rhetorical Presidency," in *Speaking to the People: The Rhetorical Presidency in Historical Perspective,* ed. Richard J. Ellis (Amherst, MA: University of Massachusetts Press, 1995).

38. Barilleaux, *The Post-Modern Presidency*, p. 49.

39. As a means of comparison, the Kingdom of Great Britain was roughly the physical size of New York and Pennsylvania combined.

40. Sidney M. Milkis, *Political Parties and Constitutional Government: Remaking American Democracy* (Baltimore, MD: The Johns Hopkins University Press, 1999), p. 14.

41. Ibid., p. 177.

42. John H. Aldrich, *Why Parties? The Origin and Transformation of Political Parties in America* (Chicago: University of Chicago Press, 1995).

43. Gregg II, "Whiggism."

44. Robert Remini, *Martin Van Buren and the Makings of the Democratic Party* (New York: Columbia University Press, 1958).

45. Sidney M. Milkis, *The President and the Parties: The Transformation of the American Party System Since the New Deal* (New York: Oxford University Press, 1993).

46. Jeffrey Tulis, "The Two Constitutional Presidencies" in *The Presidency and the Political System*, ed. Michael Nelson (Washington, DC: CQ Press, 2014), p. 14.

47. Walter Bagehot, *The English Constitution* (Portland, OR: Sussex Academic Press, 1997), p. 18.

48. Woodrow Wilson, *Congressional Government* (New York: Houghton Mifflin, 1885/1925), p. 311.

49. Ibid., p. 284.

50. Ibid., p. 54.

51. Woodrow Wilson, *Leaders of Men* (Princeton: Princeton University Press, 1952), pp. 43–44.

52. Wilson, *Leaders of Men*, p. 23.

53. Robert Alexander Kraig, *Woodrow Wilson and the Lost World of the Oratorical Statesman* (College Station, TX: Texas A&M University Press, 2004), p. 134.

54. Wilson, *Congressional Government*, p. 67.

55. Ibid., p. 69.

56. Charles Cameron, *Veto Bargaining: Presidents and the Politics of Negative Power* (New York: Cambridge University Press, 2000).

57. Neustadt, *Presidential Power*.

58. George C. Edwards III and Stephen J. Wayne, *Presidential Leadership: Politics and Policy Making* (New York: St. Martin's Press, 1990), p. 307.

CHAPTER THREE

The Historical Problems of Midterm Campaigning

The preceding chapter argued that there exists a tension at the heart of the American constitutional order between the desire for legislative predominance and the necessity of a capable executive. The (on paper) legislative predominance of the Whig Settlement and the practical legislative dominance of most early American constitutions left much to be desired, and the Constitution of the United States attempted to rectify the underlying problem. It did so by starting with the Whig Settlement of 1688 and modifying it, increasing the power of Congress (relative to Parliament) in order to ensure that the presidency could be controlled while also ensuring a sufficient independence and autonomous authority to the Office of President of the United States. As the system has been "amended" over time, additional informal barriers to presidential action have been added each time new means of presidential action were created. Thus, even changes like the rise of the modern rhetorical and administrative presidencies were contained by informal "constitutional" arrangements.

Presidential involvement in congressional campaigning—midterm or otherwise—represents a threat to that balance, because it allows for the possibility of a sizeable increase in presidential influence over their fellows in Congress, without seeing a concomitant restraint placed on subsequent presidential behavior. Through congressional campaigning, presidents can both influence who serves in Congress—threatening legislative predominance—and alter the incentives for other actors to the restrain the president—neutralizing the informal barriers built into the American order. Thus, rather than being another development that the American system of separation of powers can take in stride, presidential congressional campaigning represents a unique challenge to the traditional constitutional arrangements of the nation.

Such presidential behavior may be taken in stride today, but such was not always the case. That other actors once understood this threat can be seen in the reactions to attempts at midterm campaigning made by presidents prior to President Dwight Eisenhower. Prior to his campaign in 1954, midterm campaigns were conducted by three presidents: Andrew Johnson in 1866, William Howard Taft in 1910, and Franklin Roosevelt in 1938. Each was in a different political era, with different political norms, and each done by presidents in slightly different political situations. Yet, for all their differences the goals of each were remarkable similar, as were the results of their actions. In each of these cases, presidents set out to increase their political standing by reshuffling the congressional deck; in each case Congress struck back hard and effectively reshuffled the presidency.

The purpose of this chapter is to understand why other actors once responded to midterm campaigning with such vigor and venom, so as to better understand (in the following chapter) what has changed—that is, why it is now meekly accepted. To this end, the chapter examines each instance of midterm campaigning in some detail, laying out the situation that the president faced, what he hoped to gain, how he went about campaigning, and how Congress and other political actors behaved in response. It closes by arguing that these reactions are related to a defense of a broader political order, and that something must have changed in the 20th century to allow presidents to so blithely disregard it.

Johnson 1866

The first open presidential involvement in a midterm election took place under Andrew Johnson in 1866. President Johnson's involvement in this campaign occurred at a point of profound tension within the American polity. Dubbed by historian Howard Beale "The Critical Year," 1866 was the year in which many of the yet unresolved questions of the Civil War were to be decided.[1] The year found the North triumphant, but at a loss as to how to act in victory; the South in ruins, and uncertain how best to deal with the profound social, political, and economic changes unleashed by the conflict. Moreover, not only did tensions simmer below the surface between the North and the South, but within rival political factions of the victorious Union. It was into this political tumult that Johnson's campaign stepped.

Johnson's desire to enter the political fray was driven by a number of important factors, three of which are worth highlighting. First, he wished to definitively end the sectional crisis and, as much as possible, restore the Union to *the status quo ante bellum*.[2] The unresolved tensions of the conflict had manifested themselves in a series of political actions over the fall and winter of 1865–66. Northern antipathy to the South was shown by the refusal to seat Southern members for the session beginning in 1865. This was technically constitutional but violated the tacit understanding of what ceasing hostilities would entail—were the Southern states not members of the Union, as Congress and the Lincoln administration had always claimed? Southern recalcitrance to the reality of Northern victory was shown in the passage of the "Black Codes" in 1865 and 1866 (which Johnson tacitly supported). These laws, although they did extend civil protections to newly freed slaves and were perhaps seen as liberal in the Southern mind, from the Northern perspective reinstituted slavery under a different name.[3] Through this, Johnson walked a fine line but generally acted to favor a moderate (if nevertheless pro-Southern) vision of Reconstruction, but did not hold back in making his displeasure with the American Rump Parliament well known—and his belief that acts of that Radical-led Congress were largely illegitimate.[4]

This fight over the legitimacy of the Radical Congress played out alongside the broader fight on the nature of Reconstruction. When Lincoln was still alive he had largely gotten his way in the question of how to "readmit" the Southern states, even in the face of congressional pushback. His "Ten Percent Plan," under which a state would be readmitted on 10 percent of the voting population swearing loyalty oaths and accepting emancipation, had seen the quick formation of "acceptable" governments in several states prior to his assassination. Johnson favored continuing this rather liberal treatment of the defeated states; the Republican-led Congress did not. These differences sprang from the possession of dramatically different postwar goals. As one scholar put it, by 1865, "Johnson's war was over . . . his beloved Union had been preserved. For the Radicals military victory was incomplete without the capstone of political supremacy."[5] This differences played out in the legislative arena. Johnson's veto of a bill extending the Freedman's Bureau—and a subsequent veto of a Civil Rights Act to protect the freed slaves—shattered his connection to the party that had elected him, leaving him without clear allies in the legislature.[6] These vetoes occurred alongside a riot in New Orleans in which over forty pro-Reconstruction persons were murdered by a mob bent on a white-only political order.[7] Johnson's actions toward the bills and the riots were described by contemporaries as a "Tylerization," a reference to the disastrous presidency of Democrat turned Whig turned Democrat John Tyler a generation earlier.[8]

These fights with Congress made clear Johnson's great political weakness: he was an accidental president. Not only did he come to the office unexpectedly through Lincoln's death, Andrew Johnson came to it as a member of the "Union Party," the shell organization hoisted on the Grand Old Party (GOP) that Lincoln had formed for all pro-Union politicians during the Civil War. This might not have mattered, if not for the fact that Andrew Johnson was, and had always been, a Democrat. He was the sole Southern senator to stay loyal to the Union, and he tended to be radical in his dislike of the "slave power," but he was nevertheless a member of the partisan opposition. Thus, by early 1866, Johnson found himself elevated to the nation's highest office without a party backing him—hard to return to the Democrats after effectively abandoning them—and with an administration and Congress controlled by the other party. Moreover, one by one the members of his own administration who he thought favorable to him began to leave, upsetting his ability to use the resources of the executive branch to his favor.[9] As one scholar noted, "Bereft of a strong party organization, dealing with an independent-minded Congress, facing deep sectional division, and lacking control over patronage, Johnson desperately needed a way to build his political strength"; midterm campaigning was an obvious and valuable way he could do so.[10]

President Johnson had two connected goals that he hoped to accomplish by entering the lists of the 1866 midterm elections. First, he wished to defeat and discredit the Radical wing of the Republican Party, replacing them either with Democrats (unlikely but most favored) or moderate Republicans (likely and still acceptable). Although many Radicals had believed that Johnson, when he succeeded to the office, would be more favorable to them than Lincoln had been—because of his intense and well-documented antagonism with the planter elite—they quickly learned otherwise. Johnson certainly opposed slavery, but for the sake of the poor white and not for the slave; he did not wish to see a radical reordering of Southern life. Although the size of the Republican majority in the Congress, combined with the expulsion of the Southern (Democratic) members, made it impossible to dislodge the *party* from power, removing the more radical members would allow him to remove that *faction* from power. Consequently, he hoped that he would be able to defeat a number of the more important Radicals and thus be able to govern from the center with the moderates from both sides—or at least a sufficient number to block the seeming constancy of veto overrides.

Second, he hoped to turn this centrist coalition he believed would come into being through the midterm into a new party built around him—an echo of the Union Party that Lincoln had built during the War. Johnson hoped to pull from moderate Southerners and moderate Northerners of both parties and establish a force with which to govern.[11] He and his allies called for a convention of "National Unionists" to meet in Philadelphia on August 14, and Johnson and the bulk of his cabinet were active in promoting it—going so far as to make it clear that anyone who held a patronage position should support the movement.[12] If the new "party" was successful, it would allow the president to restrain the Radicals, provided they received enough seats to sustain the veto. More importantly, it could also be the force that would allow him to be elected in his own right in 1868. To promote this movement and this end, he set out on the first congressional campaigning in presidential history.

Johnson's campaign became known as the Swing Around the Circle. It was a railroad circuit—billed as a traditional "inspection tour" of the country—that would take him from Washington, up the coast to New York, up the Hudson Valley, across the shores of the Great Lakes, and then back east via the Ohio River by way of Saint Louis.[13] The ostensible purpose of the trip was to be present for the unveiling of a monument to Stephen Douglas in Illinois—along with a political convention in Philadelphia and a "Soldiers and Sailors Convention" in Cleveland—but it also afforded him a pretext to "show the flag" in other major cities of the northern and border states, including Baltimore, New York, Detroit, Chicago, and Louisville.[14] Moreover, railroad travel in those days involved a great number of stops between major cities, and at each stop Johnson would have the opportunity to speak. All together it afforded him the opportunity to present himself—and make his case—in a large percentage of Northern (and Radical) congressional districts.

Johnson did not make this trip alone. Rather, in the hope that the public would think of him in the same breath as them, Johnson arranged for the likes of Secretary of State William Seward, Lieutenant General U.S. Grant, Admiral David Farragut, to travel and appear with him.[15] The plan, then, was to use the trip—and the public's existing attachment to the heroes of the war—to more firmly attach the public to the accidental Johnson administration, in the hope that they might come to its rescue in the ongoing fight with Congress. That to do this might require political speech, and that public speech might be seen as unbecoming of a president, did not much faze Johnson. He had been a politician most of his adult life, and he knew what he was doing; he was also known as a knockout speaker, having spoken on his own behalf throughout his journey up the political ladder.

The "Swing Around the Circle" began on August 28, and started off better than Johnson could have hoped. Exuberant crowds met him as he traveled Maryland, Pennsylvania, New Jersey, and New York, and he made a clear but restrained case for why his administration was in the right and Congress in the wrong, and why supporters of the Union should flock to his banner.[16] But even amid this apparent success there were reasons for concern. For one, Johnson ought to have been successful in these places—the Mid-Atlantic states were far from favorable to Radical Republicanism. Additionally, he should have noticed who did not show up: the local officials of Baltimore stayed away, as did the mayor of Philadelphia, and so poor was the reception in Albany that Secretary Seward felt it necessary to admonish the sitting Republican governor for not more fully deploying the red carpet.[17] He drew well from the disaffected moderates and from the Democrats, but not from the rank-and-file Republicans who made up the majority of Northern voters.

Thus, it is not surprising that things began to move against President Johnson as the presidential train moved inland on the path of the great Yankee migration westward through the burned-over district and to the Great Lakes sections of Ohio, Michigan, and Illinois. Crowds still came out, but they were far more interested in seeing Grant, Farragut, or Seward.[18] Moreover, these crowds were less restrained and were seemingly just as interested in bantering as they were in listening. This proved a problem for Johnson. He was an extemporaneous speaker, and a good one, but his lack of notes led to trouble when he got off track, as would happen when he was repeatedly engaged by the audience.[19] Unencumbered by notes or structure, on occasions when the crowds interrupted and goaded him, Johnson had the tendency to lash out at the rabble-rousers.

This inability to tactfully deal with a less than favorable crowd became clear when the president's party reached the first openly unfavorable city, Cleveland, on September 3. When Johnson appeared, the crowd called out for Grant, but the general was "indisposed," and Johnson proceeded to speak.[20] Johnson was constantly interrupted as he spoke, particularly by cries such as "Hang [Jefferson] Davis!" The president responded by saying that rather than hanging Davis, they ought to hang Wade Phillips and Thaddeus Stevens, two senior Radical Republicans. As the crowd began to express dismay, Johnson doubled down. When some in the crowd exclaimed, "Is this dignified?" Johnson replied, "I care not for my dignity."[21] He closed out his address by reminding the public that he was the person being wronged, noting:

> In bidding you farewell I would ask you, with all the pains this Congress has taken to poison the minds of their constituents against me—what has this Congress done? Have they done anything to restore the Union of these States? No; on the contrary, they have done everything to prevent it; and because I stand where I did when the rebellion commenced, I have been denounced as a traitor. Who has suffered more, and run greater risks than I? But this factious domineering party in Congress has undertaken to poison the minds of the American people.[22]

Little did he know that he had just committed the second act for which he would later be impeached; the wheels had already fallen off the Swing Around the Circle.

Things failed to improve as the trip went on, but they reached a true nadir in St. Louis. When speaking in that city, hecklers interrupted Johnson's speech and began to shout about the recent anti-black rioting in New Orleans. In response, the speech went from bad to worse in short order. Noting that he was frequently compared to Judas, Johnson demanded to know who was his Christ—whom had he betrayed?—and declared once again that he had suffered more than many for the cause of the Union.[23] The trip never recovered from this, and though he did make subsequent stops (some far more positive), there was an evident speed with which he travelled through the Ohio Valley and back to Washington.

The trip as a whole proved especially damaging to Johnson because, as an accidental president, his greatest source of public support was the people's attachment to Lincoln. By so clearly deviating from the manner in which Lincoln had acted as both a candidate and a president, Johnson foolishly did a great deal to drive a wedge between himself and moderate supporters of the former president. The trip not only confirmed the inclinations of those who already opposed him, but pushed those on the fence—and any of the neutral press—into the arms of the Radicals.[24] The campaign was, in total, an utter fiasco.

Although it is possible that up to 1 in 10 Northern voters heard the president speak over the Swing Around the Circle, it obviously did not have the effect that President Johnson had hoped that it would.[25] Rather than drawing together a more moderate and pliable Congress, his actions had the entirely opposite result. When all the returns came in, it became clear that the Radicals had utterly triumphed, and "voters in more than 2/3 of the districts that Johnson visited during the swing around the circle voted Republican."[26] This meant that when the (Northern only) Congress reassembled the following year, the Republicans held a 179–47 advantage over the Democrats in the House and a 39–10 margin in the Senate. Johnson had failed to remember the adage "If you set out to take Vienna, take Vienna"; far from breaking the Radicals, Johnson's efforts appeared to have only made them stronger by showing them that the president had no bite.

More than this, Johnson's actions also made the Radicals furious. Johnson had taken the unprecedented step of publically attacking his congressional opponents; of suggesting they be hanged; and, most importantly, of trying to defeat them. Consequently, when the 40th Congress assembled in December of 1867, it moved quickly on a course of action everyone knew was coming: impeachment. The House voted for 11 articles of impeachment in January. Although most of the charges related to the fight over the Tenure of Office Act, the 10th article dealt directly with Johnson's speeches in Cleveland and St. Louis, noting:

> That said Andrew Johnson, President of the United States . . . did attempt to bring into disgrace, ridicule, hatred, contempt and reproach, the Congress of the United States, and the several branches thereof, to impair and destroy the regard and respect of all the good people of the United States for the Congress and the legislative power thereof, which all officers of the government ought inviolably to preserve and maintain, and to excite the odium and resentment of all good people of the United States against Congress and the laws by it duly and constitutionally enacted . . . [27]

Although Johnson survived the Senate trial and was acquitted by one vote, the damage was done.[28] Johnson's presidency, such as it was, was broken.

Congress would henceforth control Reconstruction, as the Radicals had a sufficient majority to easily override any presidential veto. Moreover, in response to vetoes of civil rights legislation, Congress passed the 14th Amendment, Southern rejection of which saw the passage of the Reconstruction Acts, which effectively granted Congress control over the former Confederacy. All together, Johnson's Swing Around the Circle was a complete failure, and far from rearranging the political landscape in his favor, his actions had furthered the cause of his opponents.

Taft 1910

The second time a president directly interfered in a midterm congressional election was not until a half-century later, in 1910, during the administration of William Howard Taft. Much like Johnson, Taft faced a political quandary early in his administration and hoped to use the midterm election to reshuffle the deck in his favor. Although Johnson's problem was relatively straightforward—he was, for all real purposes, a Democrat facing a Republican Congress—Mr. Taft's was a bit trickier, because, on the surface, it appeared that he faced no political problems. Rather than being in the minority, his presidency found the Republican Party riding high in Washington and across the country. The 1908 election saw the GOP retain the White House for a fourth straight term and strengthen its control both of Congress and of (Northern) state governments, silencing doubts about the stranglehold the party held on the polity. But, as is so often the case, that seeming dominance caused observers to look past underlying weaknesses; these weaknesses would doom Taft's attempts in 1910 and doom his presidency as a whole.

The problematic situation that Taft found himself in was a function of several different factors, but three in particular that, in combination, made the office an impossible task for him. The first major issue that Taft faced in the run-up to the 1910 midterm was the lack of any discernable political base on which to rest his administration. This is not surprising, given that Taft had never run for any elected office prior to being elected president of the United States. He had been an influential lawyer and jurist, a respected governor of the Philippines, and a successful Secretary of War—but he had never so much as run for dogcatcher. This is not to say he was not a politician—one does not rise to such major positions without being one—but he was ever a follower, never a leader. Thus, he came to the office with deep-seated convictions and a great deal of practical experience in governing, but Taft lacked the political experience—the horse trading, the vote canvassing, and so forth—that a president would find useful in the day-to-day interactions with other elected officials.[29]

This lack of a political base—and of practical political experience—was exacerbated by the fact that his presidency was effectively gifted to him.

Although he was not "accidental" in the fashion of Andrew Johnson, he might as well have been. His predecessor, Theodore Roosevelt, very easily could have run for a "third" term in 1908, but he chose not to do so. Instead, TR anointed Taft as his political heir and threw his weight behind the Taft campaign, making it clear to the public that a Taft administration was to be, effectively, a third Roosevelt term. This proved an albatross for Taft both because it established a particular set of expectations for his own administration, and hence boxed him in at the outset, and because it meant his political standing was merely an extension of Roosevelt's, leaving him a shaky foundation on which to stand.

This lack of an independent political base proved to be an intractable problem for him, because the Republican Party that Taft took command of in 1909 was beginning to fracture in dangerous ways. The fight between the mugwumps and the standpats that had threatened Republican hegemony in the generation after the Civil War was being replicated in the early 20th century in the fight between the Progressive and Old Guard wings. The Old Guard was based in the northeast and represented the continuation of the Gilded Age party, favoring the pro-business and pro-tariff policies that had been at the heart of the party since its inception. The Progressive faction—largely in the Midwest and West—represented the newer, more liberal portion of the party; its members desired to lower the tariff (which harmed the consumer) and wanted to use the power of government to control the excesses and abuses of the business system—even if that meant attacking allies of the party.[30]

The split between these groups had grown wider over the course of the Roosevelt administration, and the political prowess of Teddy Roosevelt was barely enough to hold the party together as he himself drifted ever closer to the Progressive wing.[31] Taft, however, was not nearly so politically deft as his mentor, and struggled mightily to continue this balancing act. The party split was exacerbated in the 1908 elections, when "many standpat Republicans failed to gain nomination or survived by narrow margins," further strengthening the Progressive faction.[32] This meant that as the chosen successor of the sainted Teddy, Taft was left with a series of progressive projects to continue, and he did work diligently in his first year to advance them. But though President Taft supported many progressive aims, he was also conservative by temperament, which left him much less disposed to seek progress for its own sake than his predecessor, and much more willing to compromise to get half a loaf. This was a dangerous combination of politician tendencies for someone in charge of a Republican party that was collapsing into disunion, and part and parcel of his experience as an administrator rather than a politician.

In many ways this fracturing party, combined with his lack of a secure attachment to either wing of that fracturing apparatus, left him between a rock and a hard place for the two major issues that would torpedo the first half of his presidency. The first major issue—and indeed the major issue of the late

19th and early 20th centuries—was the American (Republican) tariff system. The tariff was beloved by much of American industry—and by the Old Guard—for driving up the price of imported competition, and loathed by much of the country—and the Progressives—for unnecessarily driving up the cost of consumer goods. Although the tariff system had long been the third rail of Republican politics, Taft had campaigned on a revision (reduction) of the tariff in 1908, and he called Congress into a special session at the start of his term in order to do just that. The House bill did achieve serious reductions in the tariff rates, but the Old Guard Republican leader in the Senate, Nelson Aldrich, effectively derailed the process. Senator Aldrich tacked on 800 amendments to the House bill, taking a blanket revision and carving out a series of exemptions. Although the resulting Aldrich-Payne Act did lower rates, for the Progressives it made merely insubstantial window dressing of reform.[33] Worse for Taft, because it represented something of a White House–supported compromise, each side found fault with him for the passage of the bill—the Old Guard for even attempting to reform the tariff, and the Progressive for failing to see it through.[34]

The effective failure of tariff reform—and the subsequent recriminations—was followed in short order by a more famous event, the Pinchot Affair. In late 1909, Taft and the Secretary of the Interior, Richard Ballinger, got in a spat with Gifford Pinchot, the first chief of the United States Forest Service.[35] Pinchot had been specifically chosen by TR to carry out his conservation agenda, and he was a public symbol of the commitment by the federal government to progressive land management. Unfortunately for himself and for Taft, Pinchot believed himself to be indispensable—or at least un-removable—and so took a series of actions that effectively required that Taft remove him. This not only caused an uproar within the progressive wing of the party, but it marked the start of the collapsing relationship between Taft and the newly stateside (having returned from killing all the African wildlife he could find) Teddy Roosevelt. As the Times reported, "Pinchot Ousted; Party War On."[36]

Thus, by the dawning of 1910, President Taft found himself in an untenable position. Having come into office without a strong political base, he had quickly managed to earn the enmity of both major factions within his own party, with major figures in both camps already declaring him *persona non grata*.[37] Having taken control of a fractured party, his actions had quickly brought previously hidden fissures to the surface and broke them open wider than ever. Taft had assumed the mantle of Theodore Roosevelt, but he found himself unwilling to bear it. Put frankly, his first year in office was a political disaster, and it found him fighting an "insurgency" within the Republican Party, both in Congress and in the nation as a whole. However, Taft might have been a genial fellow, but he was no pushover; when push came to shove, he shoved right back.

President Taft hoped to use the 1910 midterms to right the ship of state and right the Republican Party by expunging those elements in the party that stood in the way of accomplishing the party's goals—that is to say, those that stood in his way.[38] The problem he faced was the strength and independence of progressive Republicans. Their intransigence and their relatively large size denied President Taft the ideologically unified party that would be able to advance his policy agenda (which was really just the Republican platform). If he could break the back of the progressive movement within the Republican Party, then he would end the divisions that wracked it. If he could end those divisions, then he could more effectively control the party on a single line of action, and thus he would be able to accomplish all the things he had promised to do in the 1908 Republican platform.

He set about his "purge" by both directly campaigning and indirectly cutting the legs out from underneath his opponents. He did this by trying to deprive them of the resources necessary to sustain them. In early 1910, he ordered his cabinet—most importantly the postmaster general[39]—to cut patronage from any member of Congress who was not a regular Republican.[40] This was not so vast a thing as it would have been prior to creation of the civil service, patronage jobs still accounted for a large portion of the federal workforce; this was a major attack at the political support of his opponents. Correspondingly, he told the Republican Congressional Campaign Committee to withhold funds from representatives and senators who stood against the administration.[41] The party was a major source of campaign funds, and Taft wanted to remind those who had forgotten that he who pays the piper calls the tune.

Unfortunately for Taft, things did not go as planned. For starters, while he was kicking his purge campaign into gear, his opponents—both in the Republican and Democratic parties—came together for a purge of their own. In early 1910, the insurgent House Republicans joined with the Democratic minority to break the power of the speakership within the chamber. On the strength of this cross-party coalition, the House voted to strip Speaker Cannon of his control over the Rules Committee, the source of his ability to dominate the chamber.[42] A primary reason for this insurrection was the intransigence of Cannon to progressive aims. Although the defeat of the Speaker did not particularly concern Taft on a personal level—he was far from a friend of Cannon's—the victory of the insurgents over the standpats further strained the bonds of the Republican Party as the election approached.

Second, Taft's campaign efforts did not go as planned. He had hoped to use the 1910 midterm election as a chance to purge the party of its more progressive members and return it to old-fashioned orthodoxy. In this President Taft failed, and in spectacular fashion. Not only did the progressive wing survive the purge, it thrived, when "forty incumbent conservatives lost to progressives in the primaries," further pushing the party to the left and driving further wedges between the party's wing.[43] Thus, when a chastened GOP returned for the next Congress (having ceded 10 Senate seats along with 57 seats and the House majority to the Democrats), it faced minority status in the lower chamber, and a Senate run by a cross party "liberal coalition." Far from breaking his congressional opponents, Taft's actions had strengthened and emboldened them, destroying any hope of major accomplishments in the second half of his term.

But worst of all, the midterm broke both the image of Republican inevitability that had hung over the country since 1896 and the vestiges of intraparty comity in the run-up to the looming 1912 presidential campaign. Within the Democratic Party, this led to ambitious politicians smelling blood and sensing that the White House was in reach for the first time in a generation. This was particularly the case for Democrats swept in on the 1910 wave, including a newly elected governor of New Jersey, Woodrow Wilson. On the Republican side, the election broke the union between Roosevelt and Taft, as a defeated Taft now threw in his lot with the Old Guard in order to have stable political backing.[44] This, in turn, pushed Roosevelt further into the arms of the progressives and fueled his insurgent-turned-outsider campaign in 1912, which saw Taft suffer the embarrassment of being the only major party candidate to ever finish third in a presidential race. Once again, interference in the midterm campaign led to presidential ruin.

Roosevelt 1938

The third and final president to engage in midterm campaigning prior to Dwight Eisenhower was Franklin Roosevelt; he ventured into these murky waters in 1938. His desire to do this is curious, as, on the surface, he faced a much different situation than either Johnson or Taft before him. FDR was not an accidental president facing a Congress locked down by the other party, like Johnson, nor was he elected on the coattails of another and bereft of an independent political standing like Taft. Rather, Roosevelt was a popular second-term president, who two years before had won a crushing electoral victory and whose party controlled not only the Congress but also the clear majority of the states. In his six years in office, he had radically transformed the American political environment, and he towered (politically) over any potential rivals. Yet even in the shadow of these many accomplishments, early 1938 found a spirit of unease hanging over 1600 Pennsylvania.

The Supreme Court, and the failure of the controversial packing plan, was the source of part of Roosevelt's discomfort. In the run-up to his 1936 reelection campaign, FDR had focused his efforts on launching the "Second New Deal," working to pass the Social Security Act and the Wagner Act, among other pieces of major legislation. However, from the perspective of the White House, each time a new progressive law passed, another was thrown out by the reactionary Supreme Court majority. As the laws in question most certainly could not have been unconstitutional, Roosevelt launched a campaign against the Court, arguing that it represented a backward and reactionary restraint on the public good. He famously proposed a law allowing the president the ability to appoint a new justice anytime an existing justice passed the age of 70. Unfortunately, this was a bridge too far for even many die-hard supporters.[45] In the face of public concern and, more importantly, rejection by more conservative members of the party, the Court packing plan was shelved. But FDR did not forget those who had refused to stand with him in support of the public good.

This slow burn of rage at those who stood in his way was redoubled in the early months of 1938 because of the failure of the Executive Reorganization Bill. This law would have reordered the executive branch to give the president a greater amount of practical control; it was, in effect, a more ambitious version of what would eventually be recommended by the Brownlow Commission. The gist of this plan was far from new and had been put forward not once, but several times, by Democratic and Republican presidents. Yet, such was the chatter over the bill that FDR felt compelled to publically announce that he did not wish to make himself a dictator, noting he had neither the inclination, nor the qualifications, nor the belief such a plan could succeed in the United States.[46] He publically backed the law; he talked through its merits; he met with members of Congress and the leadership of both chambers—but to no avail. Indeed, so strong was his support of the bill that it was known on Capitol Hill as a "'vote of no confidence' in the President."[47] Although the bill eventually squeaked through the House (a chamber which had a *246-seat Democratic majority*), it died in the Senate—and it was his own party that did it in.

These two failures made clear to Roosevelt the problem that stood in the way of accomplishing his goals, and that problem was the then existing Democratic Party.[48] Although the Party was riding high in all obvious respects, it was internally riven: it was, in many ways, a mirror of the Republican Party under Taft. It had near total control nation-wide but was split between a largely liberal Northern wing and an overwhelmingly conservative Southern wing. Moreover, and this conservative block was the foundation of the Party, and the home of most of the most senior and influential members. This meant that even though Roosevelt's partisans had huge majorities in both chambers on paper, in practice the majorities that backed the president on key issues were quite slim, as the administration knew it could not count on the votes of the Southern Democrats. Moreover, elements within the Republican Party appeared to latch on to this conflict with the hoped that it foretold the formation of a new conservative alliance that would effectively oppose the New Deal—something many Southern Democrats were not entirely against.[49]

Consequently, Roosevelt's hopes in the 1938 campaign were twofold. First, he wanted to reshape the American party system along ideological lines, by creating a responsible liberal (and by extension a responsible conservative) party.[50] By creating a clear and real ideological distinction between the two parties it would be both easier to govern (as the ruling party would share the same aspirations) and easy to engage the public (as they would be able to easily see the differences between the parties and judge them accordingly). Responsible parties along the British line were a deeply held dream of Woodrow Wilson, and as a disciple of Woodrow Wilson, FDR was a fervent believer in them too—particularly given that, as president, he would be the master of that Wilsonian responsible party. Consequently, he hoped to purge the Democratic Party of its conservative elements. Although this might ostensibly push those individuals into the hands of the Republicans, their arrival would, in turn, drive out the most liberal members of that party, who would naturally migrate to the Democrats. This would create a clear and real ideological distinction between the two parties and thus provide the public—and the political leadership—with all the benefits that a "responsible" party system has to offer.

The natural advantage of this was that a responsible Democratic Party would be responsible not only to the public but to Franklin Roosevelt (or whomever the president happened to be). As such, the idea of responsible parties was not only the culmination of the Wilsonian progressivism, but also the inversion of the Madisonian pluralism of the Constitution and the *Federalist Papers*. It would have not only uprooted the separation between the President and Congress, but also made it impractical for Congress to ever stand in the president's way—and, by extension, the Court or the states. But for Roosevelt, the impact of a responsible party system was as yet hypothetical and could only come about if the copperheads were driven from the Democratic Party.

In the spring of 1938, Franklin Roosevelt announced his intention to wade into the coming congressional contests through a "fireside chat." On June 24, Roosevelt spoke to the American public about the "Democratic Process."[51] After summing up the accomplishments of the outgoing Congress, he moved on to "a few words about the coming political primaries."[52] He then made clear that he would enter into the fray, but made clear what his place and role would be:

> As President of the United States, I am not asking the voters of the country to vote for Democrats next November as opposed to Republicans or members of any other party. Nor am I, as President, taking part in Democratic primaries.
>
> As the head of the Democratic Party, however, charged with the responsibility of carrying out the definitely liberal declaration of principles set forth

in the 1936 Democratic platform, I feel that I have every right to speak in those few instances where there may be a clear issue between candidates for a Democratic nomination involving these principles, or involving a clear misuse of my own name.[53]

This made apparent what he intended to do and why he intended to do it: it was not as a private citizen, seeking advantage, nor as a president seeking to control Congress, but as a party leader seeking to control his party. The rationale was clear: it was unfair (to the public) that men and women who ran for office as Roosevelt Democrats turned around and stymied the very efforts they have been elected to undertake; this was bad for him, it was bad for them, and it was bad for America. To remedy this situation, he told the American people that he would throw his support behind the primary candidates he believed would best represent the public, regardless of whether or not it meant crossing swords with incumbent Democrats.

It is worth highlighting that this was a purge conducted by Roosevelt and his associates, not by the Democratic Party as an institution. The Party had, in January of 1938, publically stated that it would not interfere in the results of local primaries, and the DNC chair had promised to use the Party's resources to support whoever won each of the contests.[54] The purge ran roughshod over this commitment and was carried out entirely by the "purge committee," close associates of the president who worked at various levels of the administration. As one scholar notes, it was clear that the "purge was therefore aimed not at strengthening or overhauling the party apparatus, as Roosevelt and Farley [then chair of the DNC] had done in New York State and then nationally in the late twenties and early thirties, but at shifting the center of power away from local and state organizations in favor of the White House."[55]

Roosevelt carried out the public side of his purge campaign through radio broadcast and in-person events throughout the country. He began the campaign gingerly, tacitly endorsing Senator Robert Bulkley of Ohio while not directly advising people not to vote for his opponent (George White, who introduced him at the event).[56] He was just as tactful later that day in endorsing Senator Alben Barkley of Kentucky over the candidacy of Governor "Happy" Chandler, noting that Chandler was an excellent governor but that Barkley was an excellent, experienced, and very senior senator (being the Majority Leader).[57] Indeed, FDR showed almost too much restraint when he visited Arkansas the following week, where he said nothing but polite formalities about the sitting senator, Hattie Caraway; she backed the administration on nearly everything, but he was wary of backing a losing horse.[58] Thus, the purge began far from boldly, and the president was rather taciturn in the early going.

Indeed, Roosevelt gave unalloyed support to very few challengers over the course of his purge campaign; he may have wanted to weed them out of the party, but he was cautious by temperament. But, when the president made his mind to go after a candidate, he did—niceties be damned. For example, in August, Roosevelt continued the campaign in Georgia, attempting to unseat incumbent Senator Walter George. FDR felt a special affinity for Georgia, as it was where he had his retreat at Warm Springs, and Georgians felt a special affinity toward him; this meant that he felt "no hesitation in telling you what I would do if I could vote here next month."[59] He then proceeded to list why, given the opportunity, he would not cast a vote for Senator George, though stressing his personal regard for the man, and why he "most assuredly should cast my ballot for Lawrence Camp."[60] He did this with Senator George seated next to him.

Moreover, the Roosevelt administration did not merely apply their pressure publically, but behind the scenes as well. The bevy of New Deal programs that had come into being in the prior five years supplied the White House with a potential trump card in tight races: an enormous federal work force. Over the course of the primary season and later during the general election, people noticed odd things going on with programs like the Civilian Conservation Corps (CCC). New Deal workers would openly promote and contribute to candidates. Federal money and federal jobs would flood into districts and states where Roosevelt-backed candidates were running. It was in many ways as if the election of 1938 was both part of the future—a future in which presidents held complete sway over their parties—and part of the past—a period in which the Pendleton Act did not exist, and the spoils system remained whole and unblemished. It was an all-out push by the administration, and they wanted to win no matter what.

Yet, Franklin Roosevelt was to get little reward for his efforts. Although he deployed his time, popularity, and the resources of his office to an unprecedented degree, there was nothing significant to show for it. When Election Day came, the Democratic Party was walloped from coast to coast (outside of the South), both at the national and state levels. The Republicans gained seven seats in the Senate, 81 seats in the House, and a dozen governorships; the Democratic Party still held a strong grip on American politics, but it was weakening. The Republican Party would not be going into that good night.

Moreover, the specifics aims of the purge itself were left unfulfilled. Several of the candidates that FDR has gingerly backed—such as Senator Hattie Caraway—held on to their seats, but quite a few others—such as Senator McAdoo of California—lost, diminishing the progressive brand within the Party. Moreover, the president succeeded in evicting exactly none of the conservative Senate Democrats that he had hoped to purge. The president had invested heavily in races in from Maryland to California, and in return he received almost nothing back. Indeed, the only Democrat that Roosevelt sought to purge that actually lost was a member of the House, John O'Connor of New York, and recent scholarship argues that this defeat was not a function of Roosevelt's campaign, but rather about local political changes, most notably the weakening of Tammany Hall.[61] Consequently, instead of the purified and liberal party that was willing to advance his agenda without question, Roosevelt faced an even worse quagmire than before, and now one of his own making.

Within the Congress itself, the purge cemented the divisions between the conservative and liberal Democrats, and encouraged those in the Senate to effectively caucus with seemingly resurgent Republicans. This "Conservative Coalition" of Southern Democrats and Northern Republicans would essentially control the chamber for the next generation, leaving it frequently with strong Democratic majorities only on paper. On top of this, the heavy-handedness with which the administration had used—or was thought to have used—the federal workforce during the campaign led Congress to knock out this tool of presidential power. The Hatch Act, passed by the post-purge Congress, banned federal employees from electioneering or contributing to campaigns, removing a long-standing source of presidential electoral resources. Rather than breaking his enemies, Roosevelt had emboldened them; rather than strengthening the presidency, he had seemingly weakened it.

Discussion

Prior to 1954, these were the only attempts to engage in midterm congressional campaigning, a behavior with a particular quality: because there is no presidential election, there is no way of obscuring the fact that the president is trying to interfere in the congressional election. In each of these three campaigns, the president in question sought to use his actions to master the political situation facing him, by reshaping the American party system and, by extension, the Congress. Thus, in each attempt one can see a president trying to overthrow the structure of the Jacksonian party system, which made it easier for federal actors to work together, but isolated the local and state party apparatus from presidential influence, therefore preserving the original constitutional desire that the presidency and the Congress should be thoroughly separated.

Moreover, in each of these cases you see the Congress and the party system reacting violently to presidential interference. The results of the campaigns of 1866, 1910, and 1938 were impeachment, broken presidency (and reelection), and a broken domestic presidency (and the brakes being put on domestic liberalism for a generation). In each case, members of what was, at least on paper, the president's own party acted against him in reaction to presidential interference in the prior midterm. This makes sense, as presidential involvement in these campaigns threatens Congress's independent standing with the public and, more importantly, Congress's own ability to control the party apparatus—and by extension the presidency.

There are obvious objections that could be made to this line of thought. For one, in the case of Johnson it could easily be argued that the fundamental concern of the political class was not that Johnson was campaigning, but that he was speaking publically at all. But even if that was the underlying objection, that taboo would have dissipated by the early 20th century, so it cannot have been what restrained Taft or Roosevelt. In those two cases, it could likewise be supposed that the problem that the Republican and Democratic parties had with the actions of their respective presidents was that they interfered in the primary campaigns and that such an action was a greater threat to (the independence of) members of Congress to than presidential interference in the general. This is not without merit, but it ignores the reality that failure to support a needy candidate can just as easily result in that person being purged from the party—and presidents ignore needy members in every contemporary midterm, with no censure whatsoever.

Thus, something is different, and presidents are no longer restrained in the ways that they once were. The question that we must answer then, is what has changed? Since 1954, every president has openly engaged in campaigning for members of Congress, in both midterm and presidential cycles. Yet, when they do so, there are no notes of concern, no violent reactions by the rest of the political order. Something must have happened within the political system to cause this to happen: What? Examining that question is the purpose of the following chapter.

Notes

1. Howard Beale, *The Critical Year: A Study of Andrew Johnson and Reconstruction* (New York: Harcourt, Brace, 1930).

2. Gregg Phifer, "Andrew Johnson Takes a Trip," *Tennessee Historical Quarterly* 11, no. 1 (1952): 3–22.

3. Paul H. Bergeron, *Andrew Johnson's Civil War and Reconstruction* (Knoxville, TN: University of Tennessee Press, 2011), pp. 87, 89—hereafter *Johnson and Reconstruction*.

4. Ibid., p. 97.

5. Gregg Phifer, "Andrew Johnson Argues a Case," *Tennessee Historical Quarterly* 11, no. 2 (1952): 149.

6. Hans Louis Trefousse, *Impeachment of a President: Andrew Johnson, the Blacks, and Reconstruction* (New York: Oxford University Press, 1999), p. 30.

7. Ibid., p. 38.

8. Bergeron, *Johnson and Reconstruction*, p. 101.

9. Ibid., p. 36.

10. CQ Press, *The President, the Public, & the Parties* (Washington, DC: Congressional Quarterly Press, 1997), p. 8.

11. Bergeron, *Johnson and Reconstruction*, pp. 122–25.

12. David Miller Dewitt, *The Impeachment and Trial of Andrew Johnson* (New York: The Macmillan Company, 1903), p. 111—hereafter *Impeachment of Johnson*. Although this is an excellent study of the background and the impeachment process, Mr. Dewitt appears rather "unreconstructed" in his views, diminishing the value of the source as an objective guide; NB: at the convention Johnson gave a speech about the "so-called Congress of the United States," which directly resulted in his impeachment.

13. Inspection tours were traditional activities, dating back to Washington's tenure. They were intended as non-partisan/a-political endeavors during which the president would "show the flag." Hence, while they brought the president into the public sphere, they were not generally political in character. By this I mean that presidents did not engage in public political speech on these trips, but rather appeared as the "Office of the President."

14. Forrest Conklin, "Wiping Out 'Andy' Johnson's Moccasin Tracks," *Tennessee Historical Quarterly* 52, no. 2 (1993): 124.

15. These celebrity guests, and how they were received, is well documented in the commentary of Petroleum V. Nasby (David Ross Locke), one of the premier cartoonists and satirists of the day. See, David Ross Locke, *Swinging Round the Circle or Andy's Trip West*, New York: American News Company, 1866).

16. Bergeron, *Johnson and Reconstruction*, p. 126.

17. Ibid., p. 126; Dewitt, *Impeachment of Johnson*, p. 115.

18. Ross, *Swinging*, p. 5.

19. As Johnson himself noted during the trip: "It has never been my habit to prepare speeches, but rather to take up a subject, having previously thought on it of course, and talk about it. The very idea of make a formal preparation has always disqualified me." Quoted in Phifer, "Andrew Johnson Delivers His Argument," *Tennessee Historical Quarterly* 11, no. 3 (1952): 212.

20. Dewitt, *Impeachment of Johnson*, p. 115.

21. Ibid.

22. Ibid., p. 118.

23. Bergeron, *Johnson and Reconstruction*, p. 128; Phifer's examinations of Johnson's speaking style notes that it was extraordinarily prone to biblical allusion ("Delivers Argument").

24. Garry Boulard, *The Swing Around the Circle, Andrew Johnson and the Train Ride That Destroyed a Presidency* (New York: iUniverse, 2008), p. 156.

25. Greg Phifer, "Andrew Johnson Loses His Battle," *Tennessee Historical Quarterly* 11, no. 4 (1952): 294. The author of the above piece suggests that is a failing of the trip, but reaching 10 percent of the voting population would be a tremendous accomplishment in any era.

26. Phifer, *Loses Battle*, p. 154.

27. U.S. Senate, "Impeachment of Andrew Johnson (1868)," *US Senate: Art and History*, U.S. Senate, https://www.senate.gov/artandhistory/history/common/briefing/Impeachment_Johnson.htm#3.

28. Article X never came up to vote in the Senate trial. Rather, they voted on Article XI, and then II and III—all registering the same one-vote margin of

victory for President Johnson. For a close examination of the process, see Stephen Stathis, "The Impeachment and Trial of President Andrew Johnson," *Presidential Studies Quarterly* 24, no. 1 (1994): 29–47.

29. New York Times, "The First Year," *New York Times*, March 4, 1910. In many respects, Taft was the anti-LBJ; he had a huge amount of executive experience, but no real political acumen.

30. A Washington Observer, "The Nationwide Split of Republicans: A Curious Case of History Repeating Itself," *New York Times*, January 30, 1910.

31. Stanley Solvick, "William Howard Taft and Cannonism," *The Wisconsin Magazine of History* 48, no. 1 (1964): 51.

32. Ibid., p. 52.

33. Richard G. Frederick, "William H. Taft," *First Men, America's Presidents*, ed. Barbara Bennett Peterson (New York: Nova Science Publishers, 2010), 106—hereafter *Taft*.

34. "Taft Tariff Plea Falls Flat," *New York Times*, February 13, 1910.

35. Frederick, *Taft*, p. 108.

36. "Pinchot Ousted; Party War On," *New York Times*, January 8, 1910.

37. "Kansas Done with Taft, Editor Says," *New York Times*, January 30, 1910.

38. Frederick, *Taft*, p. 111.

39. Prior to the "privatization" of the Post Office during the Nixon administration, the Postmaster General was the head of the patronage system under most presidents, in part because "local postmasters . . . remained presidential appointees until 1970." See G. Calvin Mackenzie, "Partisan Presidential Leadership: The President's Appointees," in *The Parties Respond: Changes in American Parties and Campaigns*, 4th ed., ed. L. Sandy Maisel (Cambridge, MA: Westview Press. 2002).

40. Frederick, *Taft*, p. 112.

41. Ibid.

42. Ibid., pp. 112–13.

43. Harrell et al., 2005, p. 806.

44. There is, however, strong evidence that Roosevelt worked vigorously on behalf of the regular Republican tickets throughout the country in 1910 and did not actively seek to weaken the Taft administration until after the campaign concluded. See George Mowry, Theodore Roosevelt and the Election of 1910, *Mississippi Valley Historical Review* 25, no. 4 (1939): 523–34.

45. Daniel Scroops, *Mr. Democrat: Jim Farley, the New Deal, and the Making of Modern American Politics* (Ann Arbor, MI: University of Michigan Press, 2006), p. 153—hereafter *Mr. Democrat*.

46. Walter Tuhan, "Roosevelt Says He Doesn't Aim to Be Dictator," *Chicago Times*, March 31, 1938, p. 1.

47. Milkis, *Schattschneider and the New Deal*, p. 183.

48. Susan Dunn, *Roosevelt's Purge: How FDR Fought to Change the Democratic Party* (Cambridge, MA: Harvard University Press, 2012), Chapter 1—hereafter *Roosevelt's Purge*.

49. James Patterson, "The Failure of Party Realignment in the South, 1937–1939," *Journal of Politics* 27, no. 3 (1965): 602–17.

50. Ibid., p. 7; although the notion that the purge campaign was about restructuring the Democratic Party along ideological lines is broadly accepted (and well-argued by Dunn and others), it is not unopposed. One voice in opposition is Sidney Milkis, who argues that "Roosevelt concluded that the public good and practical politics demanded that partisan politics be *transcended* rather than *restructured*," and that his purpose was focused on building the administrative state (which the conservative elements helped to block) more than it was on creating responsible parties. See Sidney Milkis, "Franklin Roosevelt and the Transcendence of Partisan Politics," *Political Science Quarterly* 100, no. 3 (1985): 480.

51. Franklin Roosevelt, "Fireside Chat 6/24/38," American Presidency Project, UC Santa Barbara, http://www.presidency.ucsb.edu/ws/index.php?pid=15662.

52. Ibid.

53. Ibid.

54. Scroops, *Mr. Democrat*, p. 166.

55. Ibid, p. 167.

56. Dunn, *Roosevelt's Purge*, p. 121.

57. Franklin Roosevelt, "Address at Covington, July 8, 1938," *American Presidency Project*, UC Santa Barbara, http://www.presidency.ucsb.edu/ws/index.php?pid=15673&st=&stl=.

58. Dunn, *Roosevelt's Purge*, p. 127.

59. Ibid., p. 157; Franklin Roosevelt, "Address at Barnesville, August 11, 1938," American Presidency Project, UC Santa Barbara, http://www.presidency.ucsb.edu/ws/index.php?pid=15520&st=&stl=.

60. Ibid.

61. Dunn, *Roosevelt's Purge*, p. 215; the impact of local political changes on this election are discussed in Richard Polenberg, "Franklin Roosevelt and the Purge of John O'Connor: The Impact of Urban Change on Political Parties," *New York History* 49, no. 3 (1968): 306–26.

CHAPTER FOUR

A Transformation in Presidential Behavior

The last two chapters have painted a clear picture of a presidential adminis-tration that is constantly seeking to reorder the political universe in order to gain mastery of its environment, but also one that is restrained in its ability to do so by the actions of external forces. The series of formal and informal fetters constructed by both the authors of the Constitution and their political successors in the early years of the American polity successfully parried the attempts of Presidents Andrew Johnson, William Howard Taft, and Franklin Roosevelt (FDR) to use their unique status within the constitutional order and standing with the public to rejigger the political order in their favor. Yet, these attempts at midterm campaigning were not only unsuccessful on a practical level—they did not lead to victories by the intended candidates—but also rebuked and rejected as illegitimate by other political elites; more recent presidents practice the same behavior without any visible concern being shown by either political elites or the mass. Moreover, whatever political transformation allowed such a dramatic change in presidential behavior had already occurred by the onset of the presidency of Dwight Eisenhower—less than two decades after the abject failure of and subsequent negative reaction to "Roosevelt's purge." This change represented a sharp and important turn in the American political order and a dramatic break from received tradition. This begs the question: What happened?

Unfortunately, although the existing literature spends a great deal of time examining presidential campaigning on behalf of Congress in general and midterm campaigning in particular, it gives almost no attention to understand-ing how and why so dramatic a change occurred. This, I would suggest, is because it does not see it as important, as it assumes any questions about midterm campaigning to be (implicitly) answered by the conceit of the modern presidency. However, this suggests that presidential engagement in midterm campaigns simply sprang into being *sua sponte*, and in so doing ignores the agency of various presidents in bringing it about. But more importantly, it denies the fundamentally relational nature of American politics—given that presidents could not campaign at one point in time, but do now, this suggests that not merely has presidential behavior changed but that the underlying political system, and the relationships that sustained it, have changed in dramatic ways as well. The task of this chapter, then, is to understand what the changes were that allowed presidents to begin campaigning in midterm elections during the mid-20th century and why subsequent presidents continued and expanded the behavior. In what follows, I show that, in large part because of a transformation of the American party system, presidents were both enabled and incentivized to engage in midterm campaigning, and hence they began and expanded this behavior.

To accomplish this, the chapter begins with an examination of the contours of presidential midterm campaigning and looks (as much as is possible) at what the literature suggests as a "cause" for the behavior. Laying out why these theories cannot explain the real nature of midterm campaigning, it argues instead that we can best understand midterm campaigning's birth and expansion as a reaction to an altered partisan and institutional environment brought about by changes to the party system over the 20th century. These changes both removed the impediments to presidential involvement and incentivized presidential actions. The chapter closes with an empirical examination of a series of factors related to party transformations, showing how they help to explain changes in midterm behaviors.

From "No" to "Yes" and from "We" to "I"

To understand the place of midterm campaigning in the American political order, we need to understand two separate but nonetheless interconnected changes: the acceptance of presidential congressional campaigning as a behavior and the emergence of the behavior in its present form. The first of these changes is understandably tough to explain because of the comparative actions of Presidents Franklin Roosevelt and Dwight Eisenhower. Roosevelt was an innovator and a powerful political figure; for all of the positives we might apply to him, Eisenhower is hardly seen in the same light. Thus, that Dwight Eisenhower should have been the president to establish midterm campaigning as a permanent facet of presidential behavior—where Roosevelt had failed—plays very much against his type. "Ike" is a figure that even today, after decades of excellent revisionist history, is still seen as apolitical and nonpartisan.[1] We all may understand that "We like Ike," but he hardly seems the one to upset the political apple cart. Yet, by succeeding where FDR failed, he certainly did so and helped establish the mode of action for all subsequent presidents.

But that Eisenhower should undertake and succeed at this task is doubly odd. This is because whereas Roosevelt was chastised for the overtly political and partisan nature of his actions, for Eisenhower the surprise was not so much that he *did* them, but that *he* did them.[2] For example, one writer who covered the campaign noted that

> the 1954 campaign ended in an atmosphere wholly unlike what had been expected. This was largely due to the changed role of President Eisenhower. He said he has no intention of going out and getting into the partisan struggle of any district or state . . . [However, after] all the polls and surveys showed the Democrats running strong, he began to wade in. At the end he was behaving like an "old pro" and waging an all out campaign on behalf of his party.[3]

Indeed, this notion of Eisenhower as the "old pro" shows just how low the bar had been set for Ike the politician. His midterm campaign came in like a lamb, with an Eisenhower fearful of divided government strenuously warning the public that if "the Congress is controlled by one political party and the executive branch by the other, politics in Washington has a field day."[4] It went out like a slightly more assertive lamb, with Ike finally being able to countenance telling voters, "Now, of course, I would like you to vote for Senator Cooper," and several other candidates besides.[5] He even managed a feat that was, no doubt, never equaled, giving his first congressional endorsement without actually mentioning the name of the candidate that he was endorsing: "I am in the district where my Congressman . . . is running. It seems to me I have a right to speak of him."[6] When he exited the stage on November 4, 1954, Eisenhower may have seemed an "old pro," but only compared to his utter amateurishness over most of his endeavors.

But no matter how timid his undertakings were in practice, taken as a whole his actions were nothing short of transformative: the die had indeed been cast, and no more would presidents abstain from interfering in congressional elections. President Eisenhower only began campaigning when in "mid-October, with clear indications that party fortunes were in peril, he belatedly responded to the pleas of party leaders."[7] He may have been talked or dragged into it, but it did happen. In total, Eisenhower would spend just over a dozen days on the trail, giving a series of remarkably vanilla and nearly nonpartisan speeches.[8] But the actions mattered far more than the content: the genie was out of the bottle, and a political rookie had managed to break a century-long taboo.

If you look only at the surface level of the expansion of midterm campaigning over the 20th century, it appears that subsequent presidents merely built on what Ike had started. As Figure 4.1 shows, midterm campaigning was a growth industry in the late 20th and early 21st centuries, reaching a peak of 79 days of campaigning in 2002. But while they may have continued the behavior, they did not continue it with the same style or even, perhaps, purpose. Just as it has grown in scope, it has also transformed in style and tenor. Eisenhower held a series of large events on behalf of the (state) party—lots of candidates and lots of citizens—and his immediate successors followed suit. However, as the 20th century wore on, presidents began to shift their behavior (see Figure 4.2)—more events, but not necessarily more candidates. Events became more specialized and specified, and a greater emphasis was placed on individual races and persons. A good example of this can be seen in the story of two weekends separated by four decades. Over the second weekend of October 1962, President Kennedy did a swing through Pennsylvania, Kentucky, Indiana, and New York. On that same weekend 40 years later, President Bush cast a wider net, vesting Florida, Georgia, Missouri, and Montana. But where Bush made only one stop at one event per state, President Kennedy held events in Aliquippa, Pittsburgh, McKeesport, Monessen, and Washington—all in Pennsylvania. President Kennedy's travels were about rallying the state party—the whole slate, from top to bottom—to victory as Democrats; President Bush's travels were just as clearly about aiding specific candidates, based on their own relationship to him.

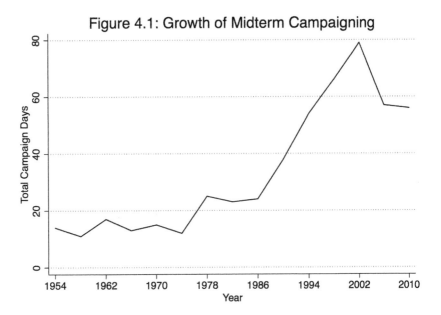

Figure 4.1: Growth of Midterm Campaigning

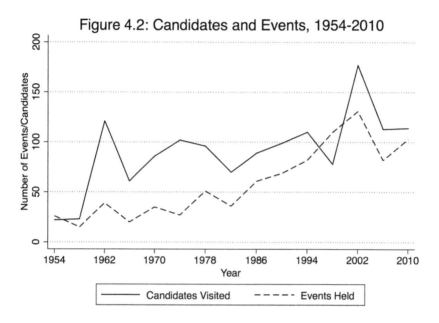

Figure 4.2: Candidates and Events, 1954-2010

Similar changes are noticeable in looking at the language used by presidents when they campaign. When initiated under Eisenhower, midterm campaigning was clearly about the importance of supporting the party and why the public would benefit from the united actions of the party as a whole. Eschewing the needs of any given individual candidate, Ike focused his speeches on the need to ensure a Republican Congress, and warned the public that if "the Congress is controlled by one political party and the executive branch by the other, politics in Washington has a field day."[9] More recent presidents have, however, effectively discarded this focus on the value of the party as a whole and have engaged in far more personalized efforts. Rather than appealing to the partisan inclinations of voters, presidents have instead sought to draw direct connections between candidates and the president, asking the American people to "make sure you send to the United States Congress a man I can work with."[10] The party-centric nature of the behavior has morphed into a president-centric vision, not only tossing the traditional vision of the party to the side, but also transforming partisan candidates going from teammates to helpers.

Taking all this into account, the rise of midterm campaigning presents two questions. First, we need to understand why President Eisenhower was able to claim the political latitude necessary to campaign in 1954 without the backlash or negative reaction from fellow political elites that had accompanied earlier midterm campaigns. Indeed, as shown above, contemporary coverage suggests that people were not surprised that he was *campaigning*, but that *he* was campaigning. Thus, we need to ascertain what changed in the 16 years between Roosevelt's purge and the 1954 elections to make midterm campaigning so broadly palatable to political elites and in such a fashion that every subsequent president (even those without his personal standing) could engage in and expand the behavior.

Second, we need to understand what changed in the political environment to allow or incentivize presidents to so radically change the behavior of midterm campaigning over the second half of the 20th century. At its inception, it was an undertaking that was seemingly other-directed and potentially altruistic, and in the early 21st century it is largely self-centered and selfish. Midterm campaigning under Obama bore resemblance to midterm campaigning under Eisenhower, but the resemblance is superficial—the extent, style, and tenor are dramatically different. Thus, we need to learn what changed to facilitate so great a change in presidential behavior, particularly given that the transformation had potentially dangerous implications for presidential partisans, let alone members of the opposition.

Misunderstood Motivations

This double transformation—from forbidden to accepted, and from other-directed to selfish—deserves explanation. Even if midterm campaigning accomplishes nothing substantive—as many scholars contend[11]—it still represents an enormous investment of time and energy by presidents, and a radical change from historical behavior. This alone ought to be understood. Unfortunately, fixated as it has been on what midterm campaigning *accomplishes*, scholarship on the presidency has largely ignored the question of why the behavior *happens* and how it has *changed*. This question is largely hand-waved away and ignored.

Still, it is not ignored entirely, and to the extent that scholarship entertains these questions, it has suggested three answers worth exploring at length. The fundamental rationale presented for this behavior is simple: presidents began engaging in midterm campaigns to elect more partisans to Congress—or at least to see fewer of them defeated. Midterm elections are notorious for the "midterm loss," and significant losses at the midterm can completely derail a presidency.[12] Though the literature is uncertain of the origins of the loss, it sensibly argues that presidents try and deflect it by attempting to create a "coattails effect" in midterm years. In presidential election years, the impact of coattails can be quite significant—"a party can expect to gain about three seats more than they would have won otherwise with every additional percentage point of the two-party vote won by the parties' presidential candidate."[13] In this telling, midterm campaigning is reactionary and designed to allow presidents a greater ability to return the most partisan Congress possible under the circumstances. It does not represent something dramatic, then, but something wholly utilitarian (if perhaps belated in inception).

Present scholarship also argues that the rise and expansion of this behavior is another symptom of political modernity and the "modern presidency." Starting with the "public" and "rhetorical" presidencies, the argument goes that having gained the accepted capacity to speak publically, and realizing that carrying it on in a permanent campaign can be helpful, presidents merely view the midterm elections as yet another opportunity to hold forth with the public and hence increase their own standing, politically and electorally.[14] As a result, these scholars argue that the reason presidents campaign in midterms is to help ensure their own reelection (and they now can do so without punishment), and they do so more often now than previously because they just like the public aspects of the presidency too much not to do so. This is an admittedly useful thesis because it provides a reason for both why presidents could campaign in 1954 but not before (public presidency) and why they expanded their campaign efforts so dramatically in more recent years (permanent campaign). Yet, in this scenario midterm campaigning is not a unique phenomenon, but simply an extension in broader trends of presidential behavior.

Third, the literature also presents a practical and materialist reason for the birth and growth of midterm campaigning, arguing that it has grown because of modern technologies for travel and communications. The replacement of the train with the plane, and the telegraph with the satellite, mean that presidents can not only engage in travel with much greater speed but can do so without losing the ability to effectively act. As Hager and Sullivan put it, "President Reagan should pursue more public activities than President Truman because Reagan can travel to more places, faster and more comfortably."[15] Samuel Kernell suggests that there might be substantial lag time in this (hence why travel does not spike immediately after the introduction of jet travel) but that it really picked up steam with the advent of outsider presidents; they, being less inclined to play inside baseball, took to the public; modern technology aided them.[16] Thus, the combination of modern technology and presidents disinclined to sit around Washington created the perfect situation for an explosion of campaign activity.

The explanations offered by the literature for the emergence and growth of midterm campaigning are entirely reasonable. It makes perfect sense that the aim of midterm campaigning is the election of more partisans and that the reason midterm campaigning came into being is reflexively straightforward: to do just that. To engage in this sort of behavior requires both practical ability and political capacity, and thus it also makes sense that midterm campaigning is the outcome of both the modern technology that makes it physically possible and the modern political order that enables it. Nevertheless, even as they appear reasonable, one can see, under a closer inspection, that each of the three reasons offered by existing scholarship suffers major flaws.

For example, to hold that presidential midterm campaigning is an outgrowth of modern methods of action embodied in the idea of the public presidency captures an important truth, but it gets us no more than halfway to understanding the reason(s) why the behavior emerged and expanded. Certainly, scholars are correct that that the acceptance of the public presidency is essential to the story of midterm campaigning—they certainly could not have done it had public speech been political suicide—but such an understanding gets us no closer to explaining why it began *when* it did. If midterm campaigning is a function of an ability and a willingness to engage with the public, then by no rights should Eisenhower have been the first to undertake the practice (successfully). Why were presidents unwilling to campaign publically in midterms when the likes of Garfield or Bryan were willing to campaign for themselves, and Teddy Roosevelt, Taft, and Wilson[17] were willing to publically fight for legislation generations earlier?[18] Likewise, in relying on the idea of the permanent campaign and the public presidency to explain the rise of midterm campaigning, we ignore the fact that the later action is a constituent part of the former two. This not only creates a reflexive definition, but it fails to approach the question concerning why presidents choose or choose not to do this—it effectively asserts it as a given.

It also makes sense to understand the birth (and expansion) of midterm campaigning through the lens of modern technology; but doing this likewise only gets us halfway home. Certainly, the use of jet-powered aircraft makes presidential travel easier, as do satellites, the Internet, and a thousand other creations. President Kennedy commented on this himself, noting in an interview given during the 1962 midterms "that by November 6 we'll have traveled more than any President and almost as much as all of them in this century in an off year, but that's partly because of jet planes."[19] However, to go from this point to a declaration that technology led to the birth of the behavior ignores and obscures key points. Presidents could travel extensively and effectively well before the creation of jet aircraft or satellite communication. Andrew Johnson's Swing Around the Circle took him up the eastern seaboard and west of the Mississippi—and back—in a few short weeks, and this was echoed in the extensive travel of presidents like Teddy Roosevelt and Woodrow Wilson. Likewise, the Air Force One of 1962 was not materially slower than its contemporary equivalent. What then about transportation technology explains the huge increase in presidential campaigning? It can make travel and campaigning easier and faster to do, but it does not *allow* it. Indeed, it may be more reasonable to see technology as something that enables modern presidents to engage in travel as freely as their predecessors, given increased demands of their office; it lowers the opportunity cost of the travel, therefore allowing them to bear the costs of their office while still engaging in heavy travel schedules. Technology allows quicker hops, and ever-present abilities to communicate, but it certainly does not explain why presidents travel, or even why they travel as much as they do.

Finally, the notion that the motivation of midterm campaigning is the same as its presumptive impact—the election of more partisans—is equally problematic, and fails to provide an adequate basis for either phase of the activity's history. It neither tells us why presidents campaign as they do or why they do so at all. On one hand, this is because existing scholarship provides answers that cannot realistically serve as solutions to the question(s) at hand. Certainly, presidents engage in midterm campaigning to help elect partisan members of Congress, to gain a more supportive Congress, to gain more electoral strength; it would only make sense, and there is strong empirical evidence to support this. Yet, admitting that fact does not get us any closer to understanding why presidents act differently today than they did 50 or 100 years ago; a more supportive Congress is not a modern dream, but something desired by every president from Washington on down. If the cause of midterm campaigning is simply that presidents want these things, then one must ask why did it not occur sooner. FDR, Truman, and indeed all presidents between Johnson and Eisenhower wanted these things and may have wanted them more given the larger historical impact of midterm losses.[20] Yet, they did not seek them in this manner. Hence, although it certainly makes sense that presidents hope that more partisans get elected because of their efforts, this cannot serve as a valid basis for why they choose to campaign (instead of pursuing other options) in the first place.

Parties All the Way Down

Although each of the above explanations for the emergence and growth of midterm campaigning over the 20th century has merit, there is another that better explains this behavior: midterm campaigning came into being as a result of the transformation of the American party system over the course of the 20th century. As noted above, the party system helps to structure the relationship between the White House and Congress, and thus helps to set the terms of cooperation and the risk/rewards of antagonism that exist between the branches. As we saw in Chapter 2, this relationship was, for much of American history, deliberately structured to restrict presidential action by incentivizing cooperation *within* the confines of the party and deliberately structuring parties to enable them to restrict aggressive presidential action.[21] However, this was upset in the past century. The 20th century—particularly the postwar period—was a period of massive upheaval within the party system of the United States, bringing about dramatic changes to a long established political order; these changes created the environment in which midterm campaigning could rise and flourish.

For this thesis to be true, the transformation of the American party system must first explain why midterm campaigning emerged when it did, and not earlier. A cursory examination of the history of American parties shows that it does so admirably. Prior to the mid-20th century, the party system in the United States was organized to disincentive presidential involvement in congressional matters (see the examples of Taft, Roosevelt, and Johnson in Chapter 3), by granting other partisan actors power within, commensurate to that of the president. This is because the American party system had, since its birth in the Jacksonian era, been designed "to constrain national administration and to engage the participation of ordinary citizens."[22] It did so in several ways. First, the system was largely decentralized, built from the bottom up, and centered at the local level. The national party apparatus existed (by at least 1856), but any attempt by presidents to centralize control was met "by the tenacity of [a] highly mobilized, highly competitive, and locally orientated democracy."[23] Thus, as noted in Chapter 2, the real partisan action was within the state and local parties, thus ensuring that local and state networks, bosses, and elites maintained the lion's share of influence within the party as a whole.

Moreover, presidential capacity to interfere within state party establishments would have been sorely limited in this period. The presidency certainly possessed resources, but Woodrow Wilson was a touch hyperbolic when he argued that, for the president, "his patronage touches every community in the United States . . . and he can go far towards establishing a complete personal domination. He can even break party lines asunder and draw together combinations of his own devising."[24]

The presidency possessed considerable tools, but they were narrow and were attached to the institution he led rather than directly to the party. This did not diminish their political value, and they could be used to devastating effect.[25] Nevertheless, the tools of the patronage system were not as well suited for the era of the public presidency. Moreover, to the extent they allowed the president to control the national party, they were of limited value—as they only allowed control of the national institution. The national party apparatus (of which they might be able to claim control) was weak and devoid of permanent resources. Local bosses, however, were truly powerful within both political and general realms. Tweed, Pendergast, and Weed—these were the individuals who controlled the working structure of the party and dispensed aid and favors to partisans. These bosses chose candidates, collected funds, and organized campaigns. Thus, each controlled his own fiefdom and represented local or state interests rather than any overarching national polity. They had no wish for external forces—presidential or other—to interfere in this dynamic. Thus, well into the 20th century, the presidency was, within the realm of party, simply another powerful actor, and not necessarily the most powerful one, and fear of upsetting powerful, established, and seemingly permanent interests likely held back presidential ambitions in this sphere.

But this too passed away, and by the 1950s the "traditional" mass-level American party system had begun to break down, as mass partisanship lessened and individuals "dealigned" from partisan affiliations.[26] At the heart of this change, it is often posited, is the rise of the welfare state.[27] As scholars have noted, "The great, mass-based parties of the nineteenth century were fueled by patronage, government jobs, contracts, and subsidies, all distributed by victorious parties," and so the modern liberal welfare state largely displaced the system's raison d'etre.[28] No longer able to distribute services through the party, local bosses were unable to control the support of the mass public. Denied the ability to distribute patronage, party leaders were unable to control their lieutenants. Denied the ability to soak public workers for campaign funds and services, the local party leadership was bereft of resources.[29] The party machines largely collapsed, and in their place presidents were eventually able to construct "national party machines able to cope with local party oligarchies."[30] This not only reordered the parties, but removed a major point of opposition to presidential actions. Unsurprisingly, presidents moved to take advantage of the opportunities this restructuring presented.

Contemporaneous to these changes in the structure of American parties, the mid-20th century also saw the beginnings of a major ideological realignment between the Republicans and Democratic parties. Coming in to the 20th century, both parties possessed strong liberal and conservative wings, highlighted by the Southern Democrats and the (northern) Republican progressives. The strength of these wings inhibited presidential action in congressional campaigning. They would have been the natural targets of presidential attention, but they were cohesive enough to punish presidential attempts to reshape the party (see the liberal coalition after 1910 and the conservative coalition after 1938). However, as the ideological centers of each party moved left and right (respectively) in the first half of the 20th century, this internal check was removed. The impact of this ideological shift can likewise be seen in the 1948 campaign and the "surprising" victory of Harry Truman over Thomas Dewey. The defection of the "Dixiecrats" (over the issue of civil rights) would have normally doomed a Democratic candidate. However, the rising strength of the northern liberal wing of the party was more than able to offset this and grant Truman his victory—and make it clear that interference could succeed without sanction. The increasing homogeneity of the parties broke another traditional restraint on presidential action, and presidents responded by acting. Coming as it did alongside the rise of the public and rhetorical presidency, this action naturally took the form of campaigning.

These changes to the structure of the American party system not only made it *possible* for presidents to campaign in midterm election without sanction, but they also *incentivized* presidents to campaign in an increasingly active and personal manner. First, the collapse of the traditional party system did more than weaken the institutional ability of parties to resist and punish presidential actions; they also removed the basis of the historical relationship between parties and candidates/office holders. Parties were mass level institutions that could deliver votes to candidates by delivering services to the partisan public. However, unable to continue to do this, the parties (as institutions) floundered. Scholars and pundits argued that parties were obsolete, but they did not vanish.[31] Rather, after a period of evolution and consolidation they reformed themselves into entities equipped for a new era.[32] State and local parties revitalized themselves first, and "national party organizations . . . reemerged from the depths . . . of the 1970s."[33] They did so by becoming service organizations—no longer built on patronage, but on institutional and electoral information.[34] They continue to help candidates in the electoral process, but in a much different fashion.

The continued collapse of the traditional party-candidate relationship also had an impact on the other side; that is, it not only caused the parties to restructure, but it caused candidates to reevaluate their place in the political universe. As parties stumbled down, partisan identification in the mass public weakened with it, leading to a rise in the number of voters who self-identified as independent. Alongside this, electoral changes, such as redistricting, displaced established party organizations and increased the incentives for candidates to individualize their campaigns, and changes in election timing weakened their capacity to enforce party voting.[35] Reforms put into place by the McGovern-Fraiser Commission, as well as changes like the passage of the Federal Election Campaign Act (FECA) in 1974, weakened the link between the party and the selection of candidates, and federal efforts to control campaign finance removed much of their monetary powers, giving it instead to outside groups with personal missions.[36] As a result, political candidates became much more independent, and rather than party loyalists, we are likely to see candidates who are "self-chosen . . . [whose] background is likely to be less in party service than in intellectual and advocacy organizations."[37] Moreover, these independent candidates were much more likely to be beholden to outside groups with personal missions, rather than parties with long-standing interests.[38]

Finally, in addition to seeing a transformation of the institutional structure of American parties, the postwar period also saw a dramatic realignment in their ideological composition and geographic basis. Demographically, the parties became more racially polarized; geographically, the South shifted to the Republicans, and the northeast to the Democrats; ideologically, the moderate middle collapsed and caused a rise in internal ideological homogeneity with the parties.[39] This accomplished one goal of Franklin Roosevelt's purge campaign of 1938, but the impact of this realignment did not necessarily create the "responsible parties" desired by early 20th-century progressives.[40] Indeed, rather than strengthening the two parties, the initial impact of this change shattered the backbone of a party system that had held up since the end of the Civil War and ushered in a dramatically different era of partisan politics—one without former long-standing taboos.

This new era may have been painful to long-existing party organizations, but it was manna from heaven to presidents, as it provided two key positives for presidents to reset the rules of American politics. First, although the rise of a more "independent" set of candidates might have weakened the capacity for the parties to control events, they correspondingly increased the ability of presidents to do so by allowing them to pick and choose whom to support. Because these candidates entered the race as individuals, raised money as individuals, and ran as individuals, there was no inherent connection between them and the local or national party leadership—meaning there were no entrenched party leaders to anger, and there was no cause for intraparty backlash (at the institutional level) if the president picked favorites or merely ignored those with whom he disagreed. Moreover, these candidates were also more likely to be beholden to outside groups; they were also more likely to be beholden to powerful individuals who backed their candidacies—individuals such as the president of the United States.

Second, the realignments of the late 20th century had the effect of opening "virgin" territories for both parties. Although this was particularly true in the case of the Republican party in the Deep South, this change meant that presidents of both parties now had the capacity to interfere in congressional races in places where their parties were traditionally weak—an unsurprisingly wide range of the country given the historically geographically focused nature of the party system. These interferences should have been welcomed, but the lack of a strong party apparatus meant that presidents had room to intervene heavily without the fear of stepping on toes, for there were no toes to be stepped on. The collapse of both the hierarchy and the old regionality of the parties made it more practical and desirable for presidents to engage in full-scale party building. Building a consistent national brand became more possible, and (again, particularly Republican) presidents were given "a chance to construct a new political majority in their image and secure for themselves a place in the history books."[41]

And party-build they did. Wearing the hat of party leader, presidents have strengthened the instructional capacities of both the national and state parties, but in a fashion that suits their own needs first and foremost. Thanks in no small part to presidential action, the parties that reemerged in the late century were not historical parties, but parties molded in the image of the president, designed to suit his needs. Thus, under presidential leadership modern parties have strengthened institutionally and developed better capacities to aid candidates and influence elections—but on presidential terms. Moreover, wearing their hat as an independent political operative, presidents seized on the relative weakness of the parties to strengthen their personal hand vis-à-vis candidates. As candidates are no longer able to rely on the parties for funding, presidents have stepped in to fill that void, providing the opportunity for large-scale fundraisers simply through the mention of presidential presence.[42] This restriction of traditional party activities and the subsequent collapse of their historical form doubly increased the valuing of campaigning in the eyes of presidents and doubly increased the necessity of such action in the eyes of candidates. Thus, the presidential capacity to aid the candidates with national resources as the party leader and with local fundraising as a popular figure has meant that opportunities for (and demand for) presidential campaigning have never been greater than in the current era.

Overall, the changes in the composition, nature, and organization of parties have left presidents with significantly greater opportunity and reason to campaign in midterm elections. The geographic and ideological transformation of the parties—ever nudged forward by presidents—opened new areas to presidential action. The contemporaneous collapse of party control over the nomination process and the rise of individualized candidates dramatically altered the potential costs of presidential involvement by removing many potential veto or pain points. Finally, the reorganization of the parties and of finance rules created a situation wherein presidents not only held many more cards than before but also one where their assistance was more necessary than ever. Thus, aided by their status as party leaders and the dramatic chance in the political landscape, late 20th-century presidents were able to engage in midterm campaigning and also provided with more than ample opportunity and reason to do so. For midterm campaigning, it is parties all the way down.

Measuring Impact

Although the changes to the American party system in the second half of the 20th century offer a more satisfying basis from which to explain the transformation of presidential behavior in midterm elections, they do not remove the basic problem: that it is difficult to approach this question empirically. As noted at the start of the chapter, the literature does not examine the question of why presidents campaign in detail; the difficulty in approaching it is likely the reason. It is particularly difficult to explain why midterm campaigning emerged in 1954, as the elections between 1938 and then are poor points of comparison.[43] Consequently, it is difficult to definitively say whether the underlying dynamics of the American order did or did not preclude midterm campaigning prior to 1954—though it certainly seems likely that by 1950 they did not.

A way around this empirical difficulty is to accept that midterm campaigning *began* and instead focus on how it has *changed*. This provides a more straightforward approach, as it is rather easier to examine whether changes to the party system have impacted the growth and change of midterm campaigning than it is to ascertain what changes allowed a behavior to begin. In fact, in this case it is positively easy to identify a major series of changes worth examining. This is because one of the primary changes to the party system was the realignment of the Democratic and Republican parties in the North and South—with the Deep South and the East and West Coasts switching allegiances. As noted in the prior section, this realignment destabilized the party apparatus within the states, providing an opening for presidential actions. As various states became more competitive over time, presidential attention should have become focused on them, both for direct congressional concerns and for longer-term state-level (legislative and gubernatorial) concerns. Thus, if the above hypothesis is correct, we should see partisan competitiveness correlated with presidential campaigning—both in a given state and in the nation as a whole.

The way to examine this empirically is through a folded Ranney Index (fRI), a modification to the traditional measure.[44] The normal Ranney Index looks at state-level control by a single party, averaging (1) the proportion of seats in the lower chamber of the legislature held by the Democratic party; (2) the proportion in the upper chamber; (3) the Democratic share of the two-party gubernatorial vote; (4) the proportion of terms of office for the governor and each chamber that the Democratic party held control. The fRI looks at interparty competitiveness rather than control. It does this by "folding" the measure such that "[Inter-Party Competitiveness] = 1—RI −0.5], where IPC is the interparty competition index and RI is the original Ranney index."[45] Consequently, this measure can capture changes to competitiveness over time, allowing an examination of the impact of realignment.

Thus, the real value of the fRI is that it allows us an easy tool with which to show the impact of partisan instability at the state level—instability driven by the collapse and rebirth of the party system after the Second World War. Figure 4.3 shows interparty competitiveness within the states in 1954. Unsurprisingly, the figure shows incredibly low levels of competition in the solidly Democratic South, but it also shows relatively low levels in traditionally Republican states such as Kansas. Put another way, in the 1950s interparty competition (at the state level) was relatively low across the nation. Figure 4.4 shows the same index in 2010; a great deal has changed. Although a large number of states were "uncompetitive" in 1954 (as judged by being below the midpoint of 0.75 on the fRI), only two remained so by 2010—both Republican-dominated states in the Plains and both just barely under the midpoint. The realignment of the parties, therefore, opened new places for potential influence, as traditional party roadblocks would not be present. By putting a greater number of states (and races) into play, the changing dynamics of the party system have increased the possibilities for presidential influence and aspirations and therefore increased the potential value of presidential travel.

If this is the case, then we should expect a more presidential travel today than in the past, as the number of states worth traveling to is greater than it once was. A simple comparison of changes in state competitiveness and the

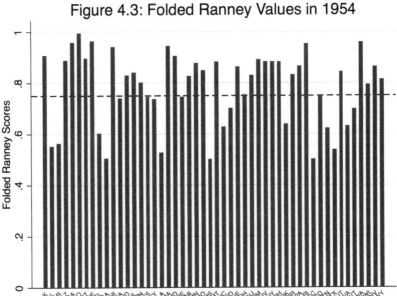

Figure 4.3: Folded Ranney Values in 1954

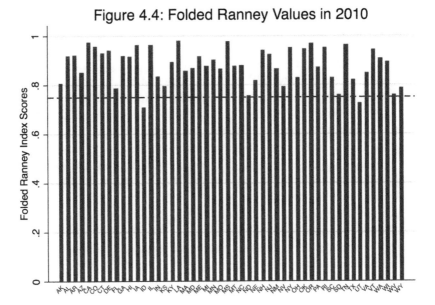

Figure 4.4: Folded Ranney Values in 2010

amount of time presidents have dedicated to campaigning shows clear evidence of midterm campaigning being driven by the party system. As Figure 4.3 shows, there is a strong, positive correlation (coming in at roughly 0.78) between the number of competitive states (those over 0.75 in the fRI) in a given midterm year and the number of days that presidents commit to campaigning. In the 1950s and 1960s, when the partisan realignment was in its infancy, there were few competitive states and little midterm campaigning, so there were only a small number of races where intervention might have been helpful. As the electoral map opened up after 1964, so too did presidential campaigning. It moved in response to the ability of presidents to influence the races and to shape their party and the polity through their actions.

This relationship between state competition and presidential travel can also be seen as presidential travel (in total number of days) per midterm cycle. The data used to examine this relationship are presented and include the number of controls that should allow effective examination of the behavior; a breakdown of the measures used is presented in Table 4.1. These data, first used in a simple ordinary least squares (OLS) model of presidential travel, presented in Table 4.2, are controls for a set of basic potential influences on congressional campaigning—things like the number and importance of House and Senate seats at issue, popularity in the present and past (vote share), and era—while also looking at the impact of state-level competitiveness. Though this type of analysis suffers from a "small-N" problem because of the limited number of midterm campaigns, the number of competitive states (those with a fRI ≥ 0.75) has a significant relationship to the amount of time that presidents spend campaigning in midterm cycles; as a greater number of states become competitive, presidents become more active in their campaigning.

Moreover, the data show that party competitiveness is distinct from other political trends and factors. For example, it would be sensible for less popular presidents to campaign less frequently and popular ones more (and they do), but as Figure 4.5 shows, although the impact of competitiveness is moderated by other factors, it maintains a significant independent impact. This gives a clearer picture of the role of competitiveness in shaping midterm campaigning: it might not determine a president's capacity for action, but it does define the field of play. Thus, the transformation of the party system in the 20th century encouraged presidential involvement in midterm election by sweeping away prior limitations, opening up the political landscape to a completely new range of possibilities.

However, as noted above, looking at this at the national level is problematic, as there are only a small number of cases because midterm campaigning has only been practiced in earnest in 15 election cycles. One way to increase the sample size but still look at the impact of changing state-level competitiveness is to change the level of focus from the nation to the state. Doing so provides a minimum of 48 cases in each cycle and allows an examination of more specific factors. When we look at presidential presence or absence from a state in a cycle—whether or not the president campaigned in a given state— we see a similar set of trends as at the national level. Just as competition drives the total campaign effort, so too do the data show it driving the likelihood of campaigning in each state.

Table 4.1 Variables and Expected Directions

Variables	Expected	Models	Type	Description
National				
Number of days campaigned	+	Presence	Count	Days campaigned in year
First term	+	Both	1/0	If it is a first term
Nixon or after	+	Both	1/0	If it is 1970 or later
Prior percent	−	Days	Continuous	Party share of presidential vote in prior election cycle
Margin in House	−	Days	Count	Partisan margin in House of Representatives
Senate seats Defending	+	Days	Count	Number of Senate seats defended by the party in that election year
Presidential popularity	+	Days	Continuous	90-day average of presidential popularity as of 1 September
Ranney states	+	Days	Count	Number of states with a folded Ranney index greater than 0.75
State				
Senate election	+	House	1/0	If there is a Senate election in state
Gubernatorial election	+	Both	1/0	If there is a governor election in state
Number of seats contesting	+	Both	Count	House races with partisans
Swing state	+	Both	1/0	If the state was within 5% in presidential election

(*continued*)

Table 4.1   (*continued*)

Variables	Expected	Models	Type	Description
Distance to capital	−	Presence	Continuous	Straight-line distance from DC to state capital
Folded Ranney Index	+	Presence	Continuous	Measure of interparty competitiveness at state level

Table 4.2   **Predicted Number of Days Campaigned**

Variables	Total Days Campaigned
Competitive "Ranney" states	0.05***
	(0.013)
Post-1970	0.40**
	(0.173)
Vote share in prior election	−0.05***
	(0.018)
Margin in House	−0.00***
	(0.001)
Senate seats defending	0.08***
	(0.016)
Presidential popularity	−0.00
	(0.006)
Constant	2.46*
	(1.270)
Observations	15
Pseudo R-squared	0.67

Robust standard errors in parentheses.
*** $p < 0.01$, ** $p < 0.05$, * $p < 0.1$.

A logit model looking at this relationship—specifically, the impact of certain factors on the probability of presidential presence within a state during a given midterm cycle—is presented in Table 4.3. As shown in these results, a number of geographic, temporal, and electoral factors play a significant role in presidential campaign travel. Presidents are more likely to travel to large, politically significant states, and they are restricted by distance and other

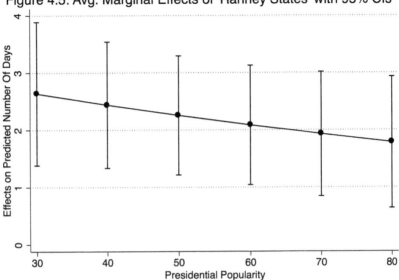

Figure 4.5: Avg. Marginal Effects of 'Ranney States' with 95% CIs

obvious factors. However, the results also clearly show a significant impact from state-level competitiveness (measure by the folded RI), such that a state that is perfectively uncompetitive (fRI of 0.5) is dramatically less likely to receive presidential attention than a state that is perfectively competitive (fRI of 1). These findings reinforce those at the national level: interparty competition, driven by destabilized parties, makes campaigning more fruitful.

This is not to say that increasing state-level competitiveness because of realignment is the only factor that matters—far from it. This can be further seen in Figure 4.6, which looks at the marginal impact of competitiveness as a function of the number of contested seats (a better measure of state size for congressional purposes than electoral votes). As it shows, the importance of state-level competitiveness falls as the size of the state increases. Presidents are going to campaign in California come hell or high water; it is simply too large, with too many races, and too much cash to be ignored. However, they may or may not come to Minnesota or Alabama, and that decision is influenced by the state's partisan competitiveness, and greatly so. This further reinforces the underlying thesis: the collapse of the prior party system in the 20th century increased the marginal value of presidential value in a huge number of congressional races; hence presidents campaigned more frequently. Competition increases the possibilities of influence and weakens the capacity for institutional pushback, and so drew presidential attention and action like moths to a flame.

Table 4.3   Predicted Presence in State

Variables	State Presence
Total campaign days	0.02***
	(0.005)
Term	0.88***
	(0.238)
Nixon or after	0.89***
	(0.277)
Distance to capital	−0.00***
	(0.000)
Folded Ranney index	1.94**
	(0.830)
Swing state	0.30
	(0.191)
Won the state	1.11***
	(0.214)
Seats contested	0.13***
	(0.020)
Senate election	0.91***
	(0.192)
Gubernatorial election	0.34*
	(0.198)
Constant	−6.31***
	(0.801)
Observations	746
Pseudo R-squared	0.26

Robust standard errors in parentheses.
*** $p < 0.01$, ** $p < 0.05$, * $p < 0.1$.

Conclusion

Public presidential involvement in congressional campaigns—midterm or otherwise—was once anathema in American politics, and presidents were rebuked and chastised for having their temerity to undertake the effort. However, in 1954—less than a generation after the failures of the seemingly far more politically savvy Franklin Roosevelt in 1938—President Dwight Eisenhower entered into the political fray of the midterm election a neophyte and

Figure 4.6: Avg. Marginal Effects of 'Folded Ranney' with 95% CIs

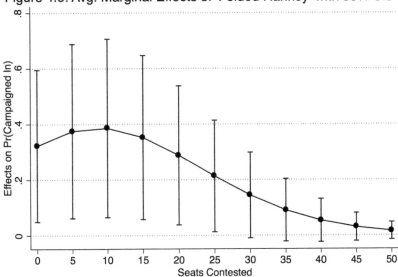

came out an "old pro." Though halting and limited when compared to our modern expectation, his actions were nonetheless important, as they ushered in a new era of presidential behavior. The purpose of this chapter has been to examine the factors that influenced the decision to enter midterm campaigning and to try to ascertain why it became accepted under and after Eisenhower and why it has exploded in scope and practice in the decades since.

Although the existing literature is not blind to this question of why presidents have chosen to engage in public midterm campaigning instead of using other political tools, it appears at best indifferent to it. To the extent that it takes up this question, the answers that it offers, while quite rational, fail to accord well with the real-world nature of this behavior. I have offered a new explanation—one consistent with the discussion of the prior chapters—of why presidents began to campaign and why they expanded their efforts so greatly: the transformation of the American party system. The dramatic changes in the nature, structure, and purpose of American parties over the course of the 20th century created a situation in which impediments to presidential actions were removed and incentives for action greatly increased. These changes confirmed presidents as the leaders of their party, granted them greater freedom of action, and made it much more useful to campaign for individual candidates.

As such, this chapter showed that it is remarkably easy to show how this party transformation has factored in to presidential decision-making. As the data built around the Folded Ranney Index showed, presidents' travel is linked to increasing interparty competitiveness in the United States. As the realignments of the postwar period open more states to both parties, presidents began to enter the fray because the increased competitiveness made their efforts increasingly worthwhile. Moreover, the data also showed that presidents are sensitive to differing levels of competitiveness between states and that states with higher levels of interparty competition at the state level are more likely to draw presidential attention. This competitiveness, an artifact of the transformation of the party system, offered the means, motive, and opportunity for greater presidential involvement in congressional campaigning.

However, as noted above, the factors motivating this behavior, though useful to know, are only useful in so far as they shed greater light on the real-world nature and impact of the behavior; that is to say, on the strategy that underpins these actions and the impact they have on the political universe. Changes to the partisan structure—reflected in altered levels of competitiveness—may induce presidential action, but they only show us what allowed presidential actions; they do not tell us what presidents hope to achieve and how they set out to do so. In the next chapter, I turn to look at how presidents plan and organize their campaign, and the extent to which the party transformation thesis manifests itself in the real-world choices of presidents on the campaign trail.

Notes

1. The gold standard of revisionist interpretation of Eisenhower remains Fred Greenstein, *The Hidden-hand Presidency* (Baltimore: Johns Hopkins University Press, 1994).

2. Admittedly, many of Roosevelt's actions (and Taft's) were materially different from Eisenhower's in that they were directed at primary elections and therefore were about overt partisan mastery. Thus, it could be argued that the reason one was forbidden and one was allowed was not due to a change in the political order, but to a change in presidential actions. However, although actively campaigning against a member of one's own party is certainly overtly hostile, much the same result could potentially be gained by simple inaction—refusal to help a fellow partisan that a president disliked. Thus, this argument overlooks the fact that as presidents should expect to lose seats at the midterm, their choice of whom they campaign for is nearly as much an expression of intraparty fighting as overt campaigning within the party primaries would be. This idea is explored in greater detail in Chapter 5.

3. Edward T. Folliard, "Republicans Appear to Be Losing House Rule," *Washington Post and Herald*, November 2, 1954, p. A1.

4. "Dwight D. Eisenhower, "Address at the Hollywood Bowl, Los Angeles, California (September 23, 1954)," in *Public Papers of the President of the United*

States: Dwight D. Eisenhower (1954) (Washington, DC: U.S. Government Printing Office, 1955), pp. 873–74—hereafter "Hollywood Bowl."

5. Dwight D. Eisenhower, "Remarks at Standiford Airport, Louisville, Kentucky (October 29, 1954)," in *Public Papers of the President of the United States: Dwight D. Eisenhower (1954)* (Washington, DC: U.S. Government Printing Office, 1955), p. 996.

6. Dwight D. Eisenhower, "Remarks at the Pennsylvania Monument, Gettysburg National Military Park" (October 23, 1954)," in *Public Papers of the President of the United States: Dwight D. Eisenhower (1954)* (Washington, DC: U.S. Government Printing Office, 1955), p. 946.

7. CQ Press, *The President, the Public, & the Parties* (Washington, DC: Congressional Quarterly Press, 1997), p. 69.

8. "Now, make no mistake, my friends. This decision is yours. Whatever your decision is is going to be loyally accepted by the people that are serving you in Washington. And I assure you, whatever your decision, no less devoted and dedicated will be my own efforts, or the executive branch's efforts, to bring about this great prosperity and more and better peace." Dwight D. Eisenhower, "Remarks at Standiford Airport, Louisville, Kentucky (October 29, 1954)," in *Public Papers of the President of the United States: Dwight D. Eisenhower (1954)* (Washington, DC: U.S. Government Printing Office, 1955), p. 1000. Quite rousing fare, no?

9. Eisenhower, "Hollywood Bowl." This is, admittedly, far from an inspiring sentiment.

10. George W. Bush, "Remarks in Auburn, Alabama" (October 24, 2002)," in *Public Papers of the President of the United States: George W. Bush (2002)* (Washington, DC: U.S. Government Printing Office, 2005), p. 1890.

11. NB: This is discussed at length in Chapter 6.

12. Inter alia, Jefffrey E. Cohen, Michael A. Krassa, and John A. Hamman, "The Impact of Presidential Campaigning on Midterm U.S. Senate Elections," *American Political Science Review* 85, no. 1 (1991): 166–78; Luke Kelle, Brian Fogarty, and James Stimson, "Presidential Campaigning in the 2002 Congressional Elections," *PS: Political Science and Politics* 37, no. 4 (2004): 827–32; Lang, Matthew, "Polls and Elections: Revisiting Midterm Visits: Why the Type of Visit Matters," *Presidential Studies Quarterly* 41, no. 4 (2011): 809–18.

13. James E. Campbell, "Predicting Seat Gains from Presidential Coattails," *American Journal of Political Science* 30, no. 1 (1986): 181.

14. Samuel Kernell, *Going Public* (Washington, DC: CQ Press, 1986); Jeffrey Tulis, *The Rhetorical Presidency* (Princeton, NJ: Princeton University Press, 1987); Sidney Blumenthal, *The Permanent Campaign: Inside the World of Elite Political Operatives* (Boston: Beacon Press, 1980).

15. Gregor Hager and Terry Sullivan, "President-Centered and Presidency-Centered Explanations of Presidential Public Activity," *American Journal of Political Science* 38, no. 4 (1994): 1085.

16. Kernell, *Going Public*.

17. Woodrow Wilson made something of an attempt at enforcing "party discipline" in the 1918 midterm election—no doubt something that was picked up on by his assistant Secretary of the Navy and ostensible protégé, Franklin Roosevelt. However, in this race Wilson limited himself to an occasional telegram, largely working with elites behind the scenes and thus effectively continuing the long-accepted, Neustadian behavior of elite bargaining. See Ronald Schurin, "The President as Disciplinarian: Wilson, Roosevelt, and Congressional Primaries," *Presidential Studies Quarterly* 28, no. 2 (1998): 409–21.

18. William D. Harpine, *From the Front Porch to the Front Page: McKinley and Bryan in the 1896 Presidential Campaign* (College Station, TX: Texas A&M University Press, 2005); Michael Korzi, "Our Chief Magistrate and His Powers: A Reconsideration of William Howard Taft's "Whig" Theory of Presidential Leadership," *Presidential Studies Quarterly* 33, no. 2 (2003): 305–24; Will Morrisey, *The Dilemma of Progressivism: How Roosevelt, Taft, and Wilson Reshaped the American Regime of Self Government* (New York: Rowman and Littlefield, 2009).

19. John F. Kennedy, "Transcript of Interview with William Lawrence, recorded for the program 'Politics—'62' (October 14, 1962)," in *Public Papers of the President of the United States: John F. Kennedy (1962)* (Washington, DC: U.S. Government Printing Office, 1963), p. 777.

20. Joseph E. Campbell, "The Presidential Surge and Its Midterm Decline in Congressional Elections, 1868–1988," *Journal of Politics* 53, no. 2 (1991): 477–87; Joseph E. Campbell, "The 2002 Midterm Election: A Typical or an Atypical Midterm?," *PS: Political Science & Politics* 36, no. 2 (2003): 203–7.

21. David Rhode, *Parties and Leaders in the Post-Reform House* (Chicago: University of Chicago Press, 1991); Jim Snyder and Timothy Groseclose, "Vote Buying, Supermajorities, and Flooded Coalitions," *American Political Science Review* 94, no. 3 (2000): 683–94.

22. Sydney M. Milkis and Jesse H. Rhodes, "George W. Bush, the Republican Party, and the 'New' American Party System," *Perspectives on Politics* 5, no. 3 (2007): 473—hereafter *New Party System.*

23. Steven Skowronek, *Building a New American State* (Cambridge, MA: Cambridge University Press, 1982), p. 40.

24. Wilson, *Constitutional Government*, p. 215.

25. For an example of how devastatingly these resources could be used, by a president not frequently given public acclaim for his political skills (as opposed to his statesmanship), look at "A. Lincoln, Politician" in David Herbert Donald, *Lincoln Reconsidered* (New York: Vintage Books, 2001), pp. 164–80.

26. Marc J. Hetherington, "Resurgent Mass Partisanship: The Role of Elite Polarization," *American Political Science Review* 95, no. 3 (2001): 619–31; Gary Cox and Jonathan Katz, "Why Did the Incumbency Advantage in U.S. House Elections Grow?," *American Journal of Political Science* 40, no. 2 (1996): 478–97.

27. Aldrich, *Why Parties?*; Morris Fiorina, "The Decline of Collective Responsibility in American Politics," *Daedalus* 109, no. 3 (1980): 25–45—hereafter *Collective Responsibility.*

28. Peri E. Arnold, "Review: TR's Puzzling Leadership," *Review of Politics* 67, no. 1 (2005): 174.

29. The relevant irony is that the prohibition on campaign involvement by federal workers (in the form of the Hatch Act) came about as a direct result of the Purge Campaign of 1938.

30. David Mayhew, *Placing Parties in American Politics* (Princeton: Princeton University Press, 1986); Pendleton Herring, *Presidential Leadership* (New Brunswick, NJ: Transaction Publishers, 2006), p. 75.

31. Fiorina, *Collective Responsibility*; David Mayhew, *Placing Parties in American Politics* (Princeton: Princeton University Press, 1986).

32. Ibid.

33. Cornelius Cotter, James Gibson, John Bibby, and Robert Huckshorn, *Party Organizations in American Politics* (Pittsburgh: University of Pittsburgh Press, 1984); Daniel Shea, "Schattschneider's Dismay: Strong Parties and Alienated Voters," in *The State of Parties: The Changing Roles of Contemporary American Parties*, 4th ed., ed. John C. Green and Rick Farmer (Lanham, MD: Rowman and Littlefield, 2003), p. 287.

34. Aldrich, *Why Parties?*

35. Gary Cox and Jonathan Katz, "Why Did the Incumbency Advantage in U.S. House Elections Grow?," *American Journal of Political Science* 40, no. 2 (1996): 478–97; Erik Engstrom and Samuel Kernell, "Manufactured Responsiveness: The Impact of State Electoral Laws on Unified Party Control of the President and House of Representatives," *American Journal of Political Science* 49, no. 3 (2005): 547–65.

36. Fiorina, *Collective Responsibility*; Richard Hall and Frank Wayman, "Buying Time: Moneyed Interests and the Mobilization of Bias in Congressional Committees," *American Political Science Review* 84, no. 3 (1990): 797–820; Jon Wright, "Contributions, Lobbying, and Committee Voting in the U.S. House of Representatives," *American Political Science Review* 84, no. 2 (1990): 417–38.

37. James L. Sundquist, *The Decline and Resurgence of Congress* (Washington, DC: The Brookings Institute, 1981), p. 371.

38. John Wright, "Contributions, Lobbying, and Committee Voting in the U.S. House of Representatives," *American Political Science Review* 84, no. 2 (1990): 417–38.

39. Edward G. Carmines and James Stimson, *Issue Evolution: Race and the Transformation of American Politics* (Princeton, NJ: Princeton University Press, 1989); Keith T. Poole and Howard Rosenthal, *Congress: A Political-Economic History of Roll Call Voting* (New York: Oxford University Press, 1997); Nolan McCarty, Keith T. Poole, and Howard Rosenthal, *Polarized America: The Dance of Ideology and Unequal Riches* (Cambridge, MA: MIT Press, 1997); Jon R. Bond and Richard Fleisher, *The President in the Legislative Arena* (Chicago: University of Chicago Press, 1992); Richard Fleisher and Jon R. Bond, "The President in a More Partisan Legislative Arena," *Political Research Quarterly* 49, no. 4 (1996): 729–48.

40. Dunn, *Roosevelt's Purge*.

41. Daniel Galvin, *Presidential Party Building: Dwight D. Eisenhower to George W. Bush* (Princeton: Princeton University Press, 2010), p. 20.

42. Aldrich, *Why Parties?*; Fiorina, *Collective Responsibility.*

43. The 1942 and 1950 midterms happened amid major wars. Although we might romanticize as such, politics certainly did not cease during them. Nevertheless, it would have been rather crass for the president to engage in such public partisan behavior during them, given the total nature of the struggle (as least in 1942). For comparison, in 1966 (Vietnam) President Johnson effectively refrained from campaigning entirely, and in 1992 (Gulf) President G.H.W. Bush was quite restrained in attacking Democrats. Likewise, in the 1946 midterm Harry Truman would have been an unpopular, accidental president—hardly someone whom candidates would have been demanding to see (in 1950 he might have been too unpopular to be of use).

44. The specifics of the folded Ranney Index, the data used to construct it, and the merits of the Ranney Index vis-à-vis other measure are discussed at length in Appendix B.

45. James D. King, "Interparty Competition in the American States: An Examination of Index Components," *Western Political Quarterly* 42, no. 1 (1989): 85.

CHAPTER FIVE

Modern Presidential Midterm Strategy

At the heart of the preceding chapter was the argument that contemporary scholarship fundamentally misunderstands the origins of presidential involvement in midterm congressional campaigns. Rather than representing a foreordained component of the modern or public presidency, the chapter argued that this behavior came about as a deliberate presidential response to an altered political landscape—the opportunity for advantage presented itself to mid-century presidents, and each successive officeholder has taken his own stab at it. Thus, the story of midterm campaigning is not one of the desires of the executive branch being functionally different in 1954 than in 1854, but rather that the opportunities available for exploitation changed, and so too did presidential behavior. Engagement in midterm campaigning represented a conscious choice to break with the tradition and the structures of the past, to seize the opportunity for greater power within and control over American political life. It is an example not of the unstoppable sweep of history, but rather of personal and institutional choice and of basic agency on the part of presidents.

But the agency that this choice represents does not extend merely to the question of whether presidents will engage themselves in a midterm campaign, but also to how the behavior is carried out—how presidents choose to run their campaign.[1] Involvement in midterm campaigning is not merely a choice between action and inaction, but between race and race, state and state, candidate and candidate. Presidential resources—most importantly time—are limited, and therefore choices must be made in their application. Whatever value presidential involvement may have for a given candidate, his assistance cannot—or at least is not—given to all candidates, let alone to all of them equally. As it has been practiced over the past 60-odd years, midterm campaigning represents a zero-sum game, with each race and each candidate competing for a finite amount of time and attention, and each donation of time and attention to one person or race reducing the availability to others. This implies that presidents ought to be strategic in their undertaking, parsing out their resources in a fashion they feel is most useful to themselves and their aims. It therefore behooves us to understand why presidents campaign in the way that they do, as this should help to show us what presidents hope to achieve by their undertakings.

Therefore, the task of this chapter is to understand what factors shape the presidential choice to involve himself in particular races over others, and the manner and method with which the president actually campaigns for the lucky few—that is, what determines the who, how, and when of midterm campaigning. In opposition to existing research, I argue that these choices are not mere reflections of external considerations such as electoral concerns—either presidential or congressional. Rather, following a line of advance similar to the preceding chapter, I argue that presidential midterm strategy is dictated by an internal desire to seize greater control over the political and partisan environment in which the presidency operates, and therefore largely driven by factors both internal to the president/presidency, and relational (between the Congress and the White House). Midterm campaigning is not a mere reaction or a mantle of leadership to which the president must, by duty of office, acquiesce, but rather an opportunity presidents have seized to reshape the Congress in their own political image. As such, they ought to do so in ways that clearly benefit themselves first and foremost, regardless of the concerns, needs, and desires of other actions and institutions.

To advance this argument, the chapter proceeds as follows. First, I present a series of simple data sets that indicate the presence of conscious choice within midterm campaigning—certainly a requirement if we are to speak of presidential strategy. Next, I examine the existing scholarship and argue that, though the literature makes valid points, there is need for a rethinking of fundamental assumptions in order to fully understand the behavior. Third, I lay out a new theory for presidential strategy, built on the idea that presidents see midterm campaigning as an opportunity for the reorganization of the political environment in which they operate, rather than merely an obligation that they must undertake. Finally, I close by examining midterm campaigning from 1970–2010 in detail, to show how candidate choice, campaign style, timing, and frequency are all explained by a presidential desire to remake the political world in his own image.[2]

The Problem

Presidents could treat each race, state, and candidate equally. They could campaign in every state, endorse every partisan, and raise every possible dollar for each and every race or for every race that met some objective and incontrovertible measure. However, even the briefest of examinations shows they do not, and simple logic (and the fact that we live in a world of scarcity) argues that they cannot. Indeed, even those presidents who commit huge amounts of time and energy to the assistance of their congressional allies do not attempt to do so in a way that treats each race or each candidate as equal. Rather, even the briefest examination of how presidents engage in midterm campaigns shows it to be an undertaking in which presidential favor is granted disproportionately to some and completely withheld from others, but in a manner that belies no overwhelmingly obvious determinants for such favor. Presidents campaign in races that their allies cannot win or lose, while ignoring close races that might benefit from assistance, and they endorse and fundraise for candidates who do not need or cannot use the assistance. This means that they are either foolish or that there is some underlying plan at work, some strategy that directs their behavior. Moreover, because they do not treat each candidate equally, it should be possible to tease out an understanding of the underlying strategy, of the reasons for which candidates they campaign for, where they do so, how they do so, and when they do so.

The questions of who and when need to be taken together, as they are linked together in the selection of candidates. Campaigning for a candidate impacts both an individual and a place, and so the choice of one candidate over another represents just as much the choice of one district or state over another. As noted in the previous chapters, midterm campaigning has been a growth industry, with presidents investing increasing amounts of time in the undertaking. Much as in the economic realm, these gains have not been shared equally, but rather been lavished on a lucky few and denied to the vast majority of partisans. As Table 5.1 shows, even as the amount of time spent campaigning has risen, the share of candidates (in this case of the House) who receive presidential attention has remained remarkably consistent and notably low. With the exception of Bush in 2002 (where coverage peaked at an astonishingly high, 44 percent of all House candidates), no president has even hit 30 percent of House races in a given cycle.

Just as importantly, there are few obvious top-level indicators as to what factors drive presidents to campaign for the candidates that they do. An examination of several potential influences is shown in Table 5.2. Although close races are more likely to draw attention, no other factor appears to be that much of a marker of presidential interest. Neither being in a large state nor a swing state makes much of an impact, and race-specific factors like the presence of

Table 5.1   Rates of Candidate Visit (House), 1970–2010

Year	Number Visited	Total Candidates	Percent Visited
1970	86	377	22.81
1974	102	377	27.05
1978	96	418	22.96
1982	70	389	17.99
1986	89	379	23.48
1990	99	388	25.51
1994	110	403	27.29
1998	78	379	20.58
2002	177	399	44.36
2006	113	391	28.90
2010	114	411	27.73

Table 5.2   Visit Rates by Factor (House), 1970–2010

Factor	Yes?(%)	No (%)
Tight Race	36.16	9.91
Senate Elec.	11.83	12.01
Large State	11.71	15.28
Swing State	9.95	13.26
Open Seat	17.77	12.93
Overall Rate	13.42	

a Senate election in the state (for a House race) are surprisingly unimportant. Even tight elections are not overwhelmingly indicative of presidential concern, as only 36 percent of those received attention.[3]

Indeed, the potentially idiosyncratic nature of this behavior is well demonstrated by an example from 1998. On September 28 of that year, President Bill Clinton spoke at a Democratic National Committee Luncheon in Rancho Santa Fe, California. Over the course of his remarks, he endorsed the candidacy of Christine Kehoe, who was running in a close race for a seat from California's 49th district.[4] During the span of the entire campaign year, President Clinton endorsed only 25 Democratic candidates for the House of Representatives—25 out of the 379 who ran. Why Christine Kehoe? Perhaps Mr. Clinton saw her as a strong candidate in a close race—she was a sitting city councilwoman and lost by only a few points to an incumbent

Republican. It might have been simply because she was running for a seat from San Diego—President Clinton campaigned more heavily in California than in any other state, spending 11 days there over the course of the campaign year. Or her endorsement could have been the result of Mr. Clinton's frenetic campaign pace in 1998—he was quite active across the length and breadth of the nation, campaigning for 66 days and holding 110 campaign events in 19 different states. But whatever it is, it is worth ascertaining why she—just like any other lucky candidate—received presidential favor, whereas the clear majority of her fellows did not.

Next, we need to understand the reasons why presidents campaign for candidates in the manner that they do. Presidents are remarkably discriminating not only in *whom* they campaign for, but in *how* they campaign for those they deign to assist. This discriminating behavior can be seen in the types of events that are held—a public ribbon cutting probably shows a lesser relationship than private fundraisers—but it can also be shown in the very way that presidents speak about candidates. This is one of the abilities of the Midterm Data Set—it allows a thorough examination of not only whom the president campaigns for but also how he actually talks about each candidate. This is important, as the way presidents speak during midterm campaigns shows a great deal more nuance than they are often given credit for. Just as presidents are evidently loath to campaign for any given candidate, let alone hold fundraisers for just any one, presidents are relatively parsimonious in use of strong language when speaking about candidates. Compare, for example, the two following statements, made within moments of each other at the same campaign event in 2002:

"We need Mitch McConnell back in the Senate. He's doing a really, really good job for the State of Kentucky."[5]

"I appreciate the fact that Geoff Davis, candidate for the U.S. Kentucky Fourth District, is with us. And Geoff, I appreciate you putting your hat in the ring."[6]

Comparing the two, it is obvious that they represent different sentiments. The former is a request that voters elect Mitch McConnell; the latter is a polite way of saying, "Thanks for coming." One shows a strong embrace of the candidate and his campaign on the part of the president; the other, rather more of a mere acknowledgment of existence. More importantly, such distinction in language as frequent and quite clear—presidents will often rattle off, "I need X, Y, and Z re-elected . . . and let's thank W for running . . ." Such distinctions, I would suggest, are far from arbitrary and, rather than being the products of random speech, suggest distinct levels of presidential interest in certain races and candidates. As such, it is obvious that not all candidates are being treated in the same way, and for no obvious reason. From the presidential perspective this talk is cheap—free, actually. Yet, presidents engage in it with high levels of sophistication and nuance—why?

The final major component of presidential strategy is the *when* of the campaign—that is temporal placement of presidential actions across the length of the campaign season. In this regard as well, candidates are treated far from equally. Figure 5.1 shows the "survival" of candidates across the 2010 midterm campaign—charting the last day in the campaign President Obama last campaigned for each candidate he interacted with over the year. As the figure indicates, far from treating every candidate equally, presidents throw many to the wayside quite early in the season, with the rest being let go at a much steeper rate as the cycle come to a close. The timing of the campaign should matter as a function of salience, and thus the value of presidential attention should not be constant across the year. Given that the public is relatively uninformed about politics, events that occur further from election day—which is to say, earlier in the year—ought to have less value, and events that are held closer ought to have greater value, as the election will become increasingly salient to the public mind as November draws closer. Thus, in the same way as frequency or style, the timing of presidential campaigning—early for some candidates and late for others—ought to act as a marker of presidential preference for some candidates over others.

Interestingly, the value of time in the campaign season is largely a presidential creation. As presidents have become more involved in midterm elections,

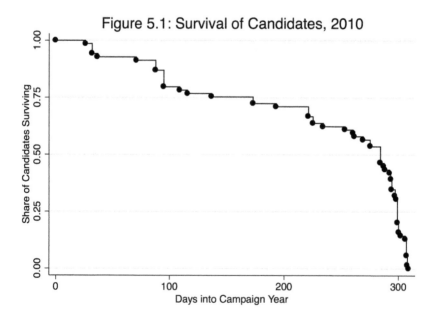

Figure 5.1: Survival of Candidates, 2010

Table 5.3   Campaign Length by Year

Year	Campaign Start	Election Day	Length of "Season"
1954	October 19	November 2	14
1958	October 27	November 4	8
1962	March 10	November 6	241
1966	June 30	November 8	131
1970	October 17	November 3	17
1974	September 18	November 4	47
1978	February 17	November 7	263
1982	March 2	November 2	245
1986	February 14	November 4	263
1990	February 8	November 6	271
1994	May 21st	November 8	171
1998	January 9	November 3	298
2002	February 27	November 5	251
2006	February 23	November 7	257
2010	January 17	November 2	289

they have not only spent more time campaigning but have begun campaigning over a greater part of the year. As Table 5.3 shows, presidents have expanded the campaign season from the traditional post–Labor Day period to an all-year affair. In doing so, they have further increased the delineation between those who receive potentially unimportant early year events and those who receive presidential support in the waning days of the campaign—such distinction mattered far less in the compressed cycle of the mid-20th century. Thus, as with who, where, and how, we must ask why it is that presidents choose to campaign when they do as well as what that choice of timing indicates about their goals and preferences.

Existing Literature

A large amount of scholarship examines the factors shaping presidential strategy within midterm campaigns, but the capacity of the existing literature to understand the factors influencing this strategy is limited. Two major issues that exist within the current literature drive this limitation. First, the literature focuses its attention on the question of candidate selection (who/where), leaving aside event choice and campaign timing. Although this

does limit its explanatory power, for our purposes it is merely an inconve-
nience, as there should be a close relationship between each of the three
choices. Presidents ought to sort from the whole universe of candidates, find
the best, and campaign for them. Timing and event choice should then be a
part of a second round of sorting, on the same principles, from this more
limited group of candidates; the best of this already reduced field will get a
better treatment. Thus, it is more a question of narrow focus than a true weakness of the literature that it fails to tackle event choice of campaign timing, and
similar factors should hold for all three.

The second and more important problem with the literature is that it is
divided into two distinct (and rather contradictory) strands of thought, each
resting on a different theoretical foundation. Indeed, the division between
these two threads is so great that the literature is clearly pulled in two very
different directions—taking the appearance, as Eshbaugh-Soha and Nicholson-
Crotty (2009) note, of "two complimentary [sic], but largely isolated bodies of
scholarship."[7] That this division exists makes sense—the discipline as a whole
lacks a clear theory of why presidents campaign in midterms, and so there
need not be any shared thread running through every bit of scholarship.
However, because this divide is so pronounced, it effectively allows each half
of the literature to don theoretical blinders and to shut out from consider-
ation myriad useful possibilities.

The first of these two threads understands midterm campaigning as a presidentially centered activity and as a subset of the larger theme of the permanent campaign. Looking at midterm campaigning in this way greatly colors
how the literature understands the basic motivations at play in midterm behaviors. As Doherty (2007) notes, "Viewing presidential actions through the lens of
the permanent campaign leads one to ascribe cynical, election-related motivations to much of what presidents do."[8] Rather than understanding presidential
actions in midterm elections as internally manufactured and driven by factors
within the election alone, the literature presumes that these behaviors become
subsumed into the broader ethos of the permanent campaign. Hence, they
are understood to be artifacts of that political truism, that the one thing every
first-term administration wants is a second one. Consequently, this batch
of the literature fixates on state factors, but those that have national political value—specifically on their value as electoral prizes. This is not to say that
these scholars treat midterm campaigning as one-dimensional or simplistic—
indeed, some argue that the "underlying strategy to a president's campaign
activity during the midterm election season that is comparable to campaigns
for the presidency itself."[9] However, by focusing so tightly on the idea of the
permanent campaign this thread of literature greatly limits its capacity for
understanding this behavior.

Driven by this focus, this scholarship centers its analysis on two principal
factors. First, it argues that presidents should and do focus their attention on

large and electorally rich states at the expense of smaller and less valuable ones. Sellers and Denton (2006) find that the electoral value of a state leads presidents to campaign there regardless of the strength or importance of the candidates therein.[10] Doherty (2007) seconds this, though with the caveat that presidents do travel to electorally poor states in a disproportionate amount to their size; and he affirms it again in (2010), though again qualifying by finding that fundraising travel may be distinct from other types.[11] Finally, Lang et al. (2011) confirm these findings, though suggesting they cannot stand apart from the odds of a president winning a particular state in the subsequent election.[12]

Second, this thread argues that presidential strategy is a function of relative (presidential) electoral strength between states. Sellers and Denton (2006) go to lengths to show the relative costs and benefits of campaigning in states given prior levels of electoral success, noting that campaigning in states where the president did poorly "may motivate voters in the opposing party to work against the president's party," while "the political costs of visiting [states he easily won] are lower"—hence, presidents should focus on states that they performed well in previously.[13] Subsequent scholarship follows this approach and looks at the impact of electoral strength broadly, such as Lang et al. (2011), who find that presidential vote share is significantly, strongly, and positively correlated with presidential travel.[14] However, it is the middle ground, the highly competitive swing states, on which the literature largely focuses—which makes sense. Doherty (2007) finds that swing state status is important for much of presidential travel, noting that the targeting of competitive states has "increased over time."[15] Likewise, Sellers and Denton (2006) find that competitive states will receive around one more day of travel per midterm than uncompetitive states.[16] Presidential travel, then, can be seen as arising from a desire to shore up support in competitive states, particularly if they are electorally important.

The second and opposing thread of the literature sees presidential strategy arising from congressional rather than presidential needs. Coming from this foundation, it sees presidential midterm actions through the lens of the traditional midterm loss. Scholars are not entirely certain where this phenomenon comes from, suggesting it might represent a cyclical tendency toward surge and decline,[17] a manifestation of changes in public opinion,[18] a form of informed retrospective voting,[19] an inherent moderation within the American public,[20] or ever a basic desire for divided government[21]—but no matter what the cause, it has cost the presidential party House (and normally Senate) seats in every midterm but three (1934, 1998, and 2002) since the Civil War.

This thread of scholarship, then, understands midterm campaigning to be evidence of a presidential desire to blunt the impact of the midterm loss by applying the resources and popularity of the presidency to individual races.

Thus, it is seen as an attempt to more or less create coattails within the midterm year. Coattails, of course, are spillovers from presidential election— "a party can expect to gain about three seats more than they would have won otherwise with every additional percentage point of the two-party vote won by the parties' presidential candidate."[22] While there may be doubt of the effect's strength,[23] the directional nature of the effect,[24] or the extent of their continuing influence,[25] it is undoubtedly an aid to presidential ambitions— and something that presidents would like to recreate in the midterm year.

Consequently, this literature sees midterm campaigning as representing a presidential attempt to make the best of a bad hand, an attempt to reverse the seemingly unbreakable trend of midterm losses by playing on his strengths and resources, by deploying them strategically to maximize results.[26] "Presidents strategically use their limited visitation resources to campaign where their personal popularity can have an additive outcome on local races"—or, more artfully put, they focus on "races where the clout of the president could make a difference."[27] Presidents focus, therefore, on races that are competitive, because that is where their actions might most easily tip the scales and hence provide the greatest return-on-investment. While also taking into account legislative success in the last Congress as well as state or national level popularity, to determine the overall extent of campaigning, the main thrust of this literature is that presidents see campaigning as a function of competitive races.[28] Candidates may be more likely to gain presidential aid if they support the president more often in Congress, and competitiveness may only impact presence with regard to certain event or race types, or even only in particular states—but it is race competitiveness that this thread of the literature sees as key.[29]

Problems with the Literature

The above examination makes one thing clear: the existing literature on midterm campaigning makes sense. It makes sense that presidents who take state politics into account would favor campaigning in California over Wyoming, or that presidents would favor traveling to a purple Florida or Ohio over a deep red Nebraska or deep blue Vermont. Moreover, it makes sense that presidents would spend their resources where they could do the most good, and thus focus on tight races over blowouts, that they would shepherd their resources in order to spend them where most needed. It makes sense, in the end, that presidents attempt to formulate a strategy based on both their own needs and desires *and* on the needs and desires of their co-partisans.

Nevertheless, though the literature suggests underlying factors that are themselves completely reasonable, it still paints a wholly incomplete picture of how presidents actually campaign. This is because, myopically focused on its two explanations, each thread of the literature sees little beyond its own interpretation, donning theoretical blinders to find exactly what it seeks. The scholarship driven by the permanent campaign imagines presidents as motivated by electoral self-interest, and so they are, and thus campaigning in the manner dictated by the ideas of the permanent campaign. The literature that assumes travel to be guided by congressional needs focuses on that possibility, and so it is, with travel predicated on the needs of candidates above all else. This is not to suggest that these finding are wrong, but that by failing to widen its gaze the literature ignores a large number of equally plausible explanations for what is going on.

The problems caused by these preconceptions can be easily seen. For example, within the thread of literature focused on the permanent campaign, the basic problem is the emphasis on the idea that campaigning is merely a function of the president's personal electoral agenda. While it may very well be that presidents use midterm campaigning to advance their own electoral needs (and we examine that possibility in the next chapter), within the data there is no (explicit) evidence that presidents actually campaign—in any way—for their *own direct* benefit instead of accruing those benefits as pleasant additions to some other more central goal. Over the last 60 years, presidents have spent over 500 days on the midterm campaign trail, and held nearly 900 public and private events. But across the entirety of the past 15 midterm election cycles, not a single dollar was raised for a president nor a single statement found in the transcripts about a president or presidential election other than errant shouts of "Four more years!" Indeed, if we look at the data, it would appear that every facet of a president's midterm campaign is other-directed—they stump for others and they raise money for others, never for themselves. Midterm campaigning may be motivated by presidential factors, but what those factors are is not readily apparent, and they are clearly additional (if not subsidiary) to factors involving the midterm elections themselves. Thus, it makes sense that what we do see in the data is presidents treating these elections as what they patently are: midterm congressional elections, midterm term gubernatorial elections, and midterm state legislative elections—not some sort of extended presidential election campaign.

It is not to say that presidents do not engage in these behaviors with an eye to strengthening themselves *in the long run*—that idea is well supported both by empirical work and by the statements of those responsible for presidential campaigning.[30] However, the weakness of the permanent campaign argument is its emphasis on midterm campaigning as a largely presidential event. Presidents may favor certain races over others because of the electoral value of a state, but those states are also the locations of key gubernatorial and senatorial races and are politically important in their own right, and presidents do not shy away from important races in otherwise insignificant states. Thus, it seem reasonable that in order to understand how state-specific factors impact campaign strategy, we surely must pay some attention to state factors that have nothing to do with the president, those things that might make states enticing even in the *absence* of presidential electoral concerns.

One such factor that should hardly need mention is that states are the places wherein congressional races occur and that certain states simply have more congressional races being contested within them. In a midterm congressional election, such a thing would seem of paramount importance. To its credit, the existing literature does not overlook this. Seller and Denton (2006) argue that competitive Senate races drive presidential presence, and Lang et al. (2011) and Eshbaugh-Soha and Nicholson-Crotty (2009) show that the number of competitive House races in the year has a substantive impact on presidential actions.[31] Still, the literature does not focus on this idea with sufficient importance: if midterm campaigns are at all congressionally driven, then one should expect as robbers to banks, so presidents to states—one to where the money is; the other to where the races are. If presidents want to elect members to Congress, then clearly there should be a great deal of influence from larger states, but only insofar as they are likewise competitive between the parties— just as predicted in the prior chapter. Yet, competitiveness aside, this literature does not look at the impact of variance in the number of (contested) races a state possesses, at least not directly.

Instead, the literature looks at this indirectly through the use of electoral votes. As these are, in the end, simply counts of a state's House and Senate delegation, they could perhaps be reasonable proxies. But I would suggest that it is a failing of scholarship that we focus on states as bearers of electoral votes rather than as bearers of congressional seats. Although the relationship between electoral votes and seats contested within the state is strong, it is far from absolute. The relationship is displayed in Figure 5.2, which shows well one of the problems of focusing on the electoral votes possessed by a state rather than congressional seats being contested within it: it ignores the historical political divisions of this country, particularly the existence of the "Solid South." Indeed, in this figure, almost every point that is significantly below the fitted line is a pre-realignment Solid South state during a Republican presidency—they frequently had large numbers of electoral votes, but they were closed for business to Republican candidates (and largely to Republican presidents). The same is true in contemporary elections for states like California or Texas—they possess large numbers of electoral votes, but the underlying congressional seats are not necessarily up for grabs by either party. Consequently, it is problematic to rely on electoral votes as a driver of midterm behavior, as they reflect electoral "values" for states that never existed, and thus a draw for presidents that never was.

Similar problems of bias can be seen within the literature focused on idea of the midterm loss as the driver of presidential action. In this case, the danger of the literature's single-mindedness is manifest in its intense regard for the importance of the *relative* competitiveness of each race. Now, as Table 5.2

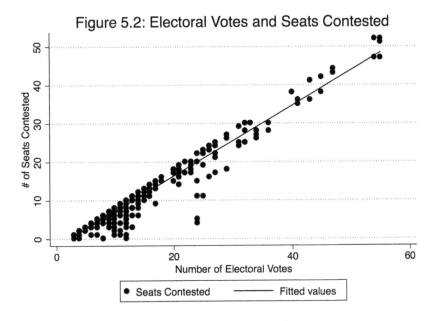

Figure 5.2: Electoral Votes and Seats Contested

made clear, the margin of a race is an important factor in presidential presence, with close races far more likely to receive attention than landslides. However, focusing on the margin of the race assumes that what presidents care about is candidate need—the demand side of the equation. Left out of this, however, is that just as important as the demand is the president's ability to supply not simply presence but influence. Influence could be many things but, at its most basic, is simply relatively electoral standing—that is, the strength of the president in the district as compared to the strength of his party's candidate in the district. If the former is greater than the latter, then the president should possess potential influence; if the opposite, then the president should possess none. If a president could not influence a race, why would he campaign in it in the first place? The extent to which the literature looks past this is striking, because the very reason the literature focuses on competitive races is that these scholars believe that presidents favor races "where the clout of the president could make a difference."[32] Hence, this thread of literature acknowledges the importance of influence, and yet its focus on congressional needs causes it to confuse a candidate factor (competitiveness) with a presidential factor (influence). This is important because, although it makes sense for a president to campaign in competitive races more than noncompetitive ones, it makes little sense for him to campaign in either if he lacks potential influence on the race.

This is not to suggest that the literature has completely ignored the importance of influence or interest, of means or motivation. Doherty (2007) suggests using prior presidential electoral strength in the state as a sign of electoral influence, Eshbaugh-Soha and Nicholson-Crotty (2009) argue for the use of state-level approval rating, and Lang et al. (2011) suggest using national approval from September of the given election year.[33] These are all valid markers of presidential strength and presidential political capital, and it is not unreasonable to assume that they are valid markers of how much potential influence a president might have, how many more voters he might be able to bring out for a candidate. However, these tell us ultimately very little about influence because influence in this case has to be inherently relative; it is not about a president being strong, but about a president being stronger. A president might have sky-high approval in a state or nationwide, but that may very well be of little concern in the planning of a midterm campaign. This is because if he is no more popular than an incumbent in a given state or district, he would likely have little chance of influencing that race, and therefore little reason to travel there. To properly understand influence, we have to understand it in the context of the relationship between the president and a candidate; we must be able to show the relative strength, the difference in strength, between the two. This is something that the literature simply does not treat.

This is a major weakness of this body of scholarship, as influence should be the fundamental requirement of president involvement. If we are to accept that "presidents strategically use their limited visitation resources to campaign where their personal popularity can have an additive outcome on local races" and that there is an "underlying strategy to a president's campaign activity during the midterm election season that is comparable to campaigns for the presidency itself," that strategy must be based on something—and influence should be at its root.[34] Campaigning in races where they lack influence should be anathematic to presidents, worse, even, than campaigning in potential blowouts. Presidents are confronted with a vast universe of potential choices in every midterm election, but to campaign effectively they need to pick and choose between them—influence should be the initial decision-making factor. Therefore, presidents should prioritize their campaign behaviors on the basis of their potential influence in given races, and greater influence should be linked to greater amounts of campaigning.

Collectively, the problem with the existing literature is that it turns itself around and focuses on presidential factors when it should look at congressional factors, and at congressional factors when it should look at presidential ones. What we need is something that bridges the divide between the congressional and the presidential, and allows us to understand them both in their proper light. We need, therefore, to turn our attention back to the party system. As we saw in the preceding chapter, changes to the party system drove the initiation and expansion of presidential midterm campaigning by altering the relationship between presidents and their co-partisans—and hence allowing the capacity to engage in campaigning in the first place. The literature does not seek to deliberately ignore parties—Sellers and Denton (2006), for example, tell us that "midterm campaigning is done by presidents in the hope of 'helping his party realize a collective goal of electing more of its members to Congress.'"[35] However, this suggests the role of the party system within midterm campaigning and, really, presidential midterm strategy is almost wholly straightforward—presidents find a group of co-partisans in need of aid and aid them. Would that it were this simple.

As we saw previously, the party system before the Second World War structured the political environment in such a way that presidents had little incentive to campaign, even if they had the ability to do so; such is no longer the case. The evolution of the American party system in the last 60 years has both encouraged this behavior and increased the necessity of presidential assistance. Consequently, the ways in which the party system structured potential midterm choices have changed as well. No longer does the party system bind and restrain presidents and restrict them to being little more than diligent and loyal members. Parties certainly structure campaign behavior, but the weakening of the American party system now structures presidential behavior in such a way as to highlight the capacity for *choice*—the ability to attempt to shape the type of party and Congress that presidents wish to interact with on the other side of the midterm election. Presidents possess agency, and they have every incentive to use it to recast the political order.

The real question, then, is what kind of Congress should presidents want to create and therefore act to create. The literature tends to suggest that this is rather straightforward—that presidents simply want to elect as many partisans as possible. This explains the emphasis on competitive races, for if the goal is simply the maximum number of partisans, then presidents should focus their efforts in the places where they can be of most value in tipping the scales of the election. Although this seems something of a truism, it ignores the very real possibility that, from the presidential perspective, some outcomes might be preferable to a maximal number of partisans. What outcome might that be? Well, all things being equal, it might very well be the case that a president might not prefer 435 members of the House and 100 members of the Senate all with the same partisan letter after their name, and instead desire the simple ability to govern in a manner he sees fit—and that merely requires 218 members of congress (MCs) and 50 (or 60) senators who share a greater commitment to his goals. While it certainly stands to reason that presidents would like more partisans in Congress, focusing on that as the outcome confuses means for ends—presidents seek to make policy, and their party is the tool to that end, not the goal. This should be particularly true of more modern presidents, who operate in a much different partisan environment—and one in which party control of the presidency is much weaker. Thus, it stands to reason that presidents may not be interested in the largest coalition in Congress, but rather the coalition most amendable to presidential desires. This would suggest a very different approach to campaign strategy.

Indeed, beyond this, the more the presidency becomes unmoored from the restraints of the party system, the more presidents should act like the Stuart and Hanoverian monarchs feared by the Whigs and their American progeny, using the resources of their office in an attempt to assemble the most favorable government they can out of the legislative body. In the American system, this would take the form of a cross-party ideological coalition—think the conservative coalition of the 1930s, 1940s, and 1950s—centered on the president. Such a coalition would not represent a party in the traditional sense, but be built to serve a particular presidential agenda, and thus need to be rebuilt by every president. Though the actual enactment of such a coalition would represent a sea change in American politics, it is not farfetched as it may seem. Indeed, President Donald Trump hinted at such a goal in the aftermath of the failure of the American Health Care Act of 2017 in the House, suggesting that he would be willing to sideline conservative Republicans (his ostensible allies) in order to bring sufficient Democrats into his congressional "coalition."[36]

All things being equal, the midterm elections—particularly the president's first midterm—are the perfect time for a president to attempt to shape both his party and such a cross-party coalition. At the midterm, a president should be at the height of his powers vis-à-vis all other partisan actors, being not only the party's "leader" and chief fundraiser, but also the nominal head of the national party, with his chosen individual running the national party machinery. So, when presented with a midterm election, with a contest featuring 500-odd congressional, senatorial, and gubernatorial races in which he is not running, in which he has no obligations, but in which his assistance, public and private, will by widely called on, are we to expect he would act in to order to simply aid partisans? Or would it be more reasonable to expect a more calculated approach, one which doles out aid in a manner that aids presidential desires, even if not wholly those of his party? I would suggest the latter.

Moreover, the political reality of the midterm cycle—that is, the likelihood of the midterm loss—suggest that presidents should act in a cross-party, ideologically focused way. Given that they ought to expect to lose seats within their own party, it would be perfectly reasonable—and politically safe—to focus their efforts on only those partisans who are most favorable to them. That is, those members of their party who are ideologically proximate. Presidents have limited time and limited resources, and they cannot campaign for everyone; who would fault them for campaigning for those partisans who are most helpful to them, even if it comes at the expense (and at the potential loss) of those fellow partisans who are furthest away?

Likewise, presidents should be relatively shy about campaigning against ideologically proximate members of the opposition. This is not to say that he would not be better served by having them replaced by (moderate) members of his own party, but that he would rather defeat more implacable members of the opposition party, as this presents a far greater reward for his efforts. But political realities make this difficult. As Figure 5.3 shows, most of any president's most intractable foes are going to be located in states or districts that are the most difficult for him to influence. Consequently, to the extent the president can reshape the opposition party, it will likely be through the defeat of those members who are already the closest to him. But, even this should be limited, as presidents should only be able to hope to replace them as their own potential influence rises.

Both of these tendencies should be influenced by which chamber is at stake in each particular race. With regards to the House, the president should have a greater ability to be selfish and unconcerned with the needs of his co-partisans. This is because there are more seats at stake (and so each is less precious); there is less chance that any given midterm will swing control of the chamber (due both to the size of majorities and the impact of gerrymandering); and there is the greater historic likelihood of losing seats in the chamber—and so less political fallout if some seats are, in fact, lost. However, in the Senate these do not hold. Few seats are at stake; majorities have, of late, been thin; and presidents have not always lost seats in the chamber—and the Senate matters more for many things the president wants to accomplish than does the House.

Putting these together, how should we expect presidents to behave with regard to midterm campaigns? Within races featuring partisan incumbents,

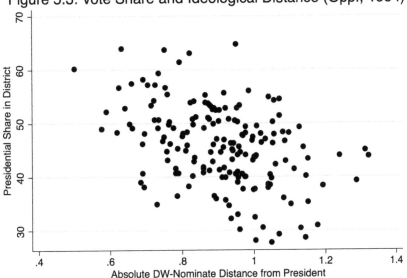

Figure 5.3: Vote Share and Ideological Distance (Opp., 1994)

we should see them act as party leaders, but with a factional bent. That is, whenever possible they should campaign for their co-partisans, if for no other reason than to "show the flag" and try and to rally support to the cause of their party. This is shown in practice, for example, in Bill Clinton spending valuable time in 1994 campaigning for party elders like Teddy Kennedy. The two were far from ideological best friends, and Kennedy went on to beat an unknown venture capitalist, Willard "Mitt" Romney, by a solid 18 points. But Clinton did show up, and more than once—why? Perhaps for many reasons, but most certainly because Teddy was a party elder, and regardless of personal feelings, his defeat would have had a far greater impact to Clinton's political fortunes than the loss of an additional Senate seat. Presidents should frequently have an incentive to campaign even if they have zero connection to or concern for the party they are a "member" of, both for the benefit of having more "supporters" in Congress and to avoid the loss of prestige that would accompany the defeat of certain candidates. As Dwight D. Eisenhower— perhaps the least overtly partisan president of modern times—reminded Americans in 1954, "When the Congress is controlled by one political party and the executive branch by the other, politics in Washington has a field day"—so make sure to vote Republican.[37]

Still, even as presidents play the party leader, they should focus their efforts on those members of their party most likely to help them in the coming term. Factions are ever present in politics and within parties— Rockefeller and Goldwater Republicans, or Blue Dog and McGovernite Democrats—and presidents should want their own faction to come out on top. This is not to say that they would place the success of their faction over that of the party as a whole. However, if, as Galvin (2010) suggests, midterm campaigning is part of a broad attempt at presidential party building, then this party building should be done to suit the desires of the president— not necessarily the "party."[38] And again, we see such behavior in the actual behavior of presidents. Whether it is Nixon, in 1970, actively campaigning *against* the candidacy of an incumbent Republican senator he deemed too liberal, or the Bush Administration throwing its weight behind the primary candidacy of Norm Coleman in 2002, presidents should have an interest in favoring partisan candidates that are aligned with them—even at the expense of offending others in their party.[39] This should be particularly true as they have greater potential influence in any given race; if they could ensure the victory of either a proximate and a distant partisan, who they ought to campaign for is obvious.

Likewise, in most situations presidents should want to avoid campaigning against proximate members of the opposition, and instead focus their attention on defeating those members who are ideologically distant from them. For example, in 2006 George W. Bush actively stayed out of the Connecticut Senate race featuring the newly independent Joe Lieberman. Even though there might have been enough Republican voters to pick up the seat in a three-way race, the certainty of Senator Lieberman—and the horror of Senator Lamont—was enough not only for Bush to abstain from campaigning but for major Republican figures to endorse Lieberman. President Reagan did this on a broader level in 1982, staying out of races involving the "Boll Weevil Democrats." In order to pass his economic plan in 1981, Reagan had promised to abstain from campaigning against any Democrat who supported it.[40] He kept his promise even though these likely represented the easiest Democratic seats to pick up.

But in both of these situations, you had relatively weak presidents—for both Reagan and Bush this was near the nadir of their presidency. Had they been more popular, more influential, who knows what might have happened? Presidents should certainly favor an opposition party that is ideologically proximate over one that is ideologically distant, but that does not mean they do not see the advantage to having more partisans over more opposition members. Thus, in the same way presidents ought to be increasingly favorable to their most ideologically proximate partisans as their influence rises, so they ought to be increasingly willing to campaign against proximate opponents as their capacity to replace them increases. This, of course, all has to happen at the margin of influence. Republicans would rather face an opposition of Blue Dogs than McGovernites—and vice versa—but they should also prefer RINOs (Republicans in name only) to Blue Dogs, provided they have the means to see them elected.

Examining Presidential Strategy

As noted above, I want to examine three types of campaign behavior: the type of presidential involvement, the frequency of that involvement, and the timing of that involvement. These require three different sets of models because they are looking at three different types of data. Presidential involvement is a binary question: Was the president present in the race? Did he endorse the candidate? Did he hold an event for the candidate? These questions require logistical regression models looking at the probability that the president would choose to campaign (in a given way) for a given candidate. Looking at frequency involves count data, and so the use of Poisson regress; timing can either make use of survival models or (as I choose) logistical models looking at the probability of campaigning in a given window. It is important to note that these two sets of models are "subsequent" to those looking at presence, and use the type of campaign presence within their own structure.

The data used for these models are described in detail in Table 5.4 and are, for the most part, straightforward. However, it should be noted that also all the data herein are data about the *incumbent members* at the time of the

Table 5.4   Variables and Expected Directions

Variables	Expected	Models	Type	Description
National				
No. of Days Campaigned	+	Both	Count	Days campaigned in year
First Term	+	Both	1/0	If it is a first term
Nixon or After	+	Senate	1/0	If it is 1970 or later
State				
Senate Election	+	House	1/0	If there is a Senate election in state
No. of Seats Contesting	+	Both	Count	House races with partisans
Race				
Open Seat	+	Both	1/0	If the contested seat is "open"
Freshmen Incumbent	+	House	1/0	If the seat has a freshmen incumbent
Race Margin	–	Both	Continuous	Final margin in the race
Party	+	Both	1/–1	Party of present incumbent
Relative Strength	+	Both	Continuous	Difference in vote percentage between candidate and president
Rank	+	Both	Continuous	The ideological distance of a given member relative to the president and his peers— proximate partisans and distant opponents have low scores

election. Hence, if it is a race in which a candidate from the president's party is challenging an incumbent of the opposition party, the data used to describe the race come from that incumbent member of the opposing party. Likewise, in situations where the seat is open (but not newly created), it means that the data refer to someone who is not even running for that seat during that election. This is obviously not the optimal way of approaching this situation, but I think it preferable to alternate possibilities for several reasons.

First, it would be a dicey exercise to attempt to formulate some type of data for candidates challenging incumbents—their ideological position, for example.

It might be possible to do so, and it might not, but even if it were, it would require no small amount of guesswork. It may be the case that presidents have a feel for factors such as the ideological placement of challenging candidates—particularly of their own party—but we as scholars have zero access to such information. Moreover, contrasting such a measure from post-hoc data would both implicitly limit examination to those challengers who happened to win election and would ignore the possibility that they did not find themselves on a sort of partisan or ideological "road to Damascus" between the campaign and when such post-hoc data become available.

Second, I used the data in this way because it seems more reasonable than not that presidents are making their campaign choices based on what they see as the status quo ante, rather than predictions about subsequent results. That is, to the extent that a president wishes to campaign for an incumbent from his party, it is on the basis of what that member has done up to that point, and not what he may do in the future. Likewise, in deciding whether to attempt to unseat a member of the opposing party, it seems logical that a president would assume that any potential member of his party would be closer to him politically and ideologically than any member of the opposition, and so what matters is which members of the opposition the president would most like to be rid of himself. For both of these reasons (and others), it seemed more reasonable to make use of incumbent data than to pursue other possibilities.

But turning to the models themselves, let us first look at presence in a given race. I speculated in the prior section that campaign presence should be a function of the relationship the president has with both the race and the candidate(s) in that race; in other words, that presidents should want to campaign where they can be effective and where their capacity to be effective could bring about a desirable result—namely, the election of candidates that will be most favorable to their own worldview. When we analyze the data, it becomes clear that this is indeed the case, though, as predicted, more so in the House than in the Senate.

Table 5.5 presents the results of the presence models for House candidates (1970–2010), looking at simple "presence" (appeared at an event with a candidate), "endorsement" (spoken, public endorsement of the candidate, per the guidelines in Appendix A), and "event for" (held an event specifically for the candidate, again per Appendix A). As it shows, many factors contribute significantly to the presidential decision to involve themselves in a given race, but those factors matter in different degrees depending on the level of involvement. For a president's simple appearance—"thanks for running"—the biggest impact comes from party status; if the race in question has a partisan incumbent, the president is fairly likely to make an appearance, but not otherwise. The races in which presidents give endorsements are influenced, on the other hand, by race-specific factors such as the

Table 5.5 Event Choice, House

Variables	Appear	Endorse	Event For
Total Campaign Days	0.01***	0.00	0.06***
	(0.002)	(0.003)	(0.010)
Senate Election	0.26***	0.47***	−0.13
	(0.100)	(0.145)	(0.350)
Seats Contesting	−0.02***	−0.04***	−0.02
	(0.004)	(0.007)	(0.016)
Open Seat	0.35**	1.04***	0.64
	(0.147)	(0.166)	(0.422)
Freshmen Incumbent	0.30**	0.59***	0.12
	(0.120)	(0.152)	(0.414)
Current Margin	−0.02***	−0.05***	−0.10**
	(0.004)	(0.009)	(0.045)
Party	2.85***	1.74***	3.36**
	(0.267)	(0.324)	(1.698)
Relative Strength	0.02***	0.02***	0.02
	(0.004)	(0.005)	(0.014)
Rank	0.01***	0.01***	0.02*
	(0.002)	(0.002)	(0.009)
Party*Rank	−0.01***	−0.01***	−0.02
	(0.002)	(0.002)	(0.010)
Constant	−3.66***	−2.95***	−9.65***
	(0.301)	(0.372)	(2.046)
Observations	4,636	4,636	4,636
Pseudo R-squared	0.15	0.17	0.23

Robust standard errors in parentheses.

*** $p < 0.01$, ** $p < 0.05$, * $p < 0.1$.

presence of a Senate race in the state and the freshmen status of the incumbent, presidents are more likely to campaign in states where there are Senate races, and freshmen members are frequently the most vulnerable. Finally, presidents appear the most likely to hold personal events (either public or private) for close races in which the incumbent is a partisan. This is not surprising, but helps to show the partisan distinction in presidential thinking that I discussed above.

An important factor in all three cases is the "Rank" variable, a self-created measure that ranks each incumbent on the value that his or her race ought to have for the president; for members of the president's party, the most ideologically proximate member is ranked as 1, and the number increases with each more distant member; for the opposition, the most ideologically distant member is ranked 1, and it increases as the members become more proximate. The idea behind this is that the president should not see each potential victory (or defeat) as equal, but rather ought to favor (all else equal) proximate members of his own party and seek to defeat distant members of the opposition. Still, as discussed above, this should be tempered by the fact that proximate members of the opposition are frequently the easiest to defeat and that an extra partisan (however moderate) is generally better than an extra member of the opposition.

This turns out to be the case if you look at the marginal influences on presidential behavior. Figure 5.4 shows the average influence of Rank at various values of Relative Strength—that is at various levels of potential influence—for both partisans and opponents. It clearly demonstrates that as potential influence on the race increases, presidents become significantly less likely to campaign for distant members of their own party and significantly more likely to campaign against members of the opposition—particularly ideologically proximate members who should be the easiest to defeat. This is reinforced by Figure 5.5, which looks at the predicted likelihood of campaigning in races featuring the closest partisan and most distant opponent versus races with a distant partisan and a proximate opponent. It shows how greatly the spread increases with influence, with differences in the probability of campaigning between proximate and distant partisans growing beyond 20 percent at positive

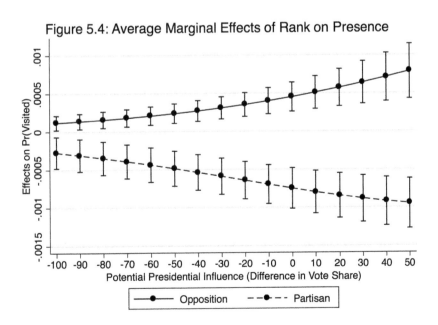

Figure 5.4: Average Marginal Effects of Rank on Presence

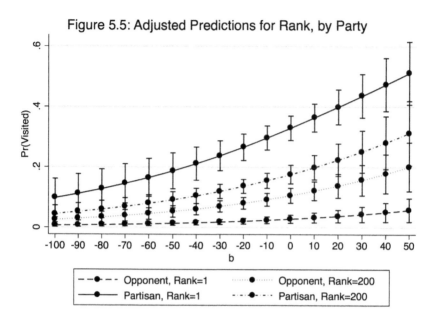

Figure 5.5: Adjusted Predictions for Rank, by Party

levels of potential influence. At least in the House, presidents play favorites within their party and increasingly focus their efforts on the most vulnerable members of the opposition as their influence grows.

The results for campaign presence for Senate candidates are presented in Table 5.6. The results bear some similarity to those reported above but also make clear that the Senate is a different animal. For all three levels of activity, presidential behavior is far more likely to be influenced by race-specific factors than it is for corresponding House races. The status of the seat (open or held), the margin in the race, and the strength of the president in the state relative to the incumbent matter far more than they do for the House, and they crowd out other factors. This makes sense because Senate races are simply more likely to be engaged with—there are fewer of them, and they are more individually and institutionally important. Consequently, it is no surprise that presidents approach them for different reasons.

None of this is to say that Senate campaigning is different than expected. Far from it, in fact. As Figure 5.6 shows, the relative importance of Senate races influences presidential presence just as it does for House races, though in a more subdued fashion. As the graph indicates, there is a divergence in the impact of "Rank" between partisans and opponents as potential influence increases—it is merely far less impactful and significant than it is in the House. Nevertheless, it suggests again that as presidential influence over a race increases, presidents will use it to favor particular races—those with proximate

Table 5.6   Event Choice, Senate

Variables	Appear	Endorse	Event For
Total Campaign Days	0.01*	0.01	0.03***
	(0.006)	(0.006)	(0.007)
Senate Margin	−0.04	−0.05**	−0.04
	(0.026)	(0.026)	(0.030)
Seats Contested	0.06***	0.06***	0.03**
	(0.019)	(0.018)	(0.013)
Open Seat	0.80***	0.58**	0.59*
	(0.283)	(0.291)	(0.312)
Current Margin	−0.09***	−0.10***	−0.11***
	(0.021)	(0.024)	(0.032)
Party	1.00**	0.91*	−0.21
	(0.493)	(0.502)	(0.613)
Relative Strength	0.05***	0.05***	0.09***
	(0.015)	(0.016)	(0.020)
Rank	0.03	0.03	−0.02
	(0.029)	(0.029)	(0.040)
Party*Rank	−0.10**	−0.09**	0.06
	(0.043)	(0.044)	(0.055)
Constant	−2.78***	−2.62***	−6.20***
	(0.936)	(0.954)	(1.177)
Observations	379	379	379
Pseudo R-squared	0.20	0.21	0.22

Robust standard errors in parentheses.

*** $p < 0.01$, ** $p < 0.05$, * $p < 0.1$.

partisans and those with members of the opposition who can be most easily defeated and replaced.

This disparity between the House and the Senate is amplified when we look at the factors influencing campaign timing, such that no models appear significant in explaining presidential timing in Senate races. In the House, however, timing appears similar to presence—the better dates are given to the "better" candidates and races. As noted above, there are several different ways to look at timing; Table 5.7 presents a pair of models. The first is a logistic regression model looking at "survival" to the last month of the campaign season. To "survive" a candidate has to have some type of presidential event in

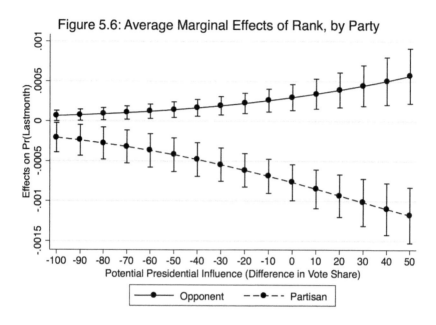

Figure 5.6: Average Marginal Effects of Rank, by Party

that period—the last month of the last week. The second is an ordinary least squares (OLS) regression model looking at the "late date" that a candidate was campaigned for, with the last date being taken from a standardized campaign year 310 days in length with 310 being Election Day—thus, a higher number reflects a final event closer to Election Day.

These results show that presidents do campaign later in the campaign year—at presumably more salient and therefore more valuable times for particular races. Namely, they favor races with partisan incumbents, close races, and states where there is a corresponding Senate race—all what we would expect. More importantly, they also care about their political relationship with the race/candidates. They campaign later for races where they have more potential impact, and they once again "favor" proximate members of their own party and attack the most vulnerable members of the opposition. This is shown well in Figure 5.6, which shows the relative impact of "Rank" at different levels of influence; as influence goes up, presidents shift their attention more fully to proximate partisans and against marginal opponents. Likewise, Figure 5.7 looks directly at a proximate and distant member of the president's own party and shows that at any given level of influence presidents are roughly twice as likely to campaign for the most ideologically proximate member of the House than they are for a distant one. This is both statistically and practically significant, as it shows the extent to which the presidents attempt to shape the makeup of their party.

Table 5.7   Event Timing, House

Variables	Last Month Logistic	Last Day OLS
Total Campaign Days	−0.00	0.18***
	(0.003)	(0.067)
Senate Election	0.51***	10.41***
	(0.128)	(2.742)
Seats Contesting	−0.02***	−0.62***
	(0.005)	(0.098)
Open Seat	0.58***	19.27***
	(0.159)	(5.811)
Freshmen Incumbent	0.14	10.44**
	(0.145)	(4.230)
Current Margin	−0.02***	−0.42***
	(0.005)	(0.101)
Party	2.51***	66.65***
	(0.286)	(5.545)
Relative Strength	0.02***	0.24***
	(0.004)	(0.075)
Rank	0.01***	0.06***
	(0.002)	(0.021)
Party*Rank	−0.01***	−0.27***
	(0.002)	(0.040)
Constant	−3.33***	17.63***
	(0.322)	(5.317)
Observations	4,636	4,636
(Pseudo) R-squared	0.12	0.10

Robust standard errors in parentheses.

*** $p < 0.01$, ** $p < 0.05$, * $p < 0.1$.

The last facet of strategy that I want to look at is the frequency of presidential campaigning on behalf of a given candidate, specifically the total number of days that the president spends campaigning on their behalf. Although there is the argument to be made that we should look at the number of events rather than the number of days, this unnecessarily prejudices the data in favor of states that are heavily populated and in which that population is dispersed—namely Texas and California. These are really the only states in which you get consistent intra-state travel on the same day, in part due to the fact

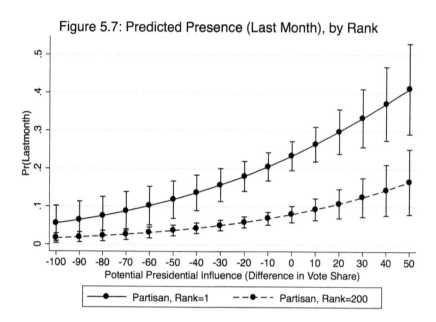

Figure 5.7: Predicted Presence (Last Month), by Rank

that congressional districts in those states can be so geographically dispersed. Thus, I feel that total days is a truer reflection of the commitment to a given candidate, while total events better reflects a presidents concern with given state.

Be that as it may, Table 5.8 shows the results of a Poisson model for both House and Senate candidates. As they show, both are heavily influenced by the by national and state-level factors as well as by the closeness of the race itself. However, as with presence and timing, the frequency with which presidents campaign in House races is also heavily impacted by the relationship between the president and the incumbent. As Figure 5.8 shows, there is a stark divide between how presidents treat partisan and opposition incumbents, and how they deal with proximate and distant candidates. As expected, these results are rather different in Senate races—shown in Figure 5.9— with a much smaller different existing between partisans and opposition members.

In total, the data strongly support the hypothesis of this chapter, that presidential strategy is dedicated to creation of a Congress and a party (system) that is the most amendable to presidential desire. Presidents made an appearance, campaigned at more valuable times, and campaigned at more frequent times for a particular set of individuals—those in their own party that are the closest to them ideologically, and those in the opposition that,

Table 5.8   Frequency of Campaigning

Variables	House	Senate
Total Campaign Days	0.01***	0.02***
	(0.002)	(0.002)
Senate Margin		−0.01
		(0.011)
Senate Election	0.27***	
	(0.082)	
Seats Contesting	−0.02***	0.03***
	(0.003)	(0.005)
Open Seat	0.21*	0.30***
	(0.110)	(0.113)
Freshmen Incumbent	0.25***	
	(0.095)	
Current Margin	−0.01***	−0.07***
	(0.003)	(0.012)
Party	2.70***	0.33
	(0.243)	(0.231)
Relative Strength	0.01***	0.03***
	(0.003)	(0.007)
Rank	0.01***	0.01
	(0.001)	(0.016)
Party*Rank	−0.01***	−0.04*
	(0.002)	(0.022)
Constant	−3.91***	−2.29***
	(0.267)	(0.439)
Observations	4,636	379
Pseudo R-squared	0.14	0.19

Robust standard errors in parentheses.
*** $p < 0.01$, ** $p < 0.05$, * $p < 0.1$.

regardless of their own ideologically proximity, are the easiest to defeat. In so doing, the president has the potential to "purge" his own party of recalcitrant members and pick up additional support through the defeat of weaker opponents—strengthening his hold over both the Congress and his own party.

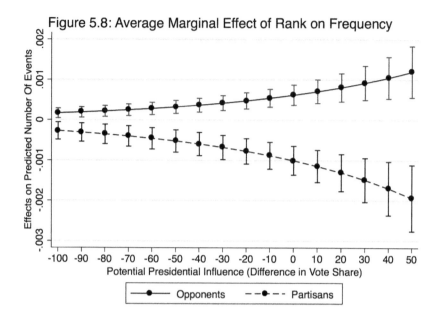

Figure 5.8: Average Marginal Effect of Rank on Frequency

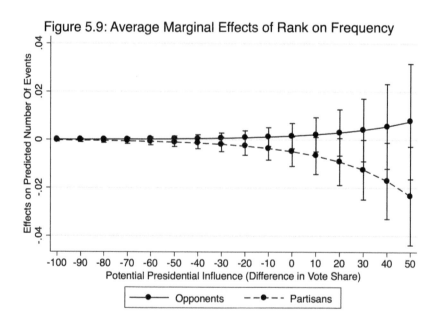

Figure 5.9: Average Marginal Effects of Rank on Frequency

Conclusion

Over the part 60 years of the behavior, presidents have campaigned heavily in midterm elections, and increasingly so. However, even as their commitment of time and energy has expanded, the actual number of candidates for whom they campaign has remained relatively small. Strong candidates in close races get ignored, and weak candidates in blowouts get notices. Some states see only one candidate visited from the entire ticket, while others are home to seemingly endless presidential events. There is, then, some sort of strategy at work, some sort of decision making process through which sorts out how, when, and where presidents campaign. As both an interesting empirical question in itself and because of the importance it could have for understanding American government, it bears understanding why presidents favor the candidates they do and what factors structure presidential midterm campaigns.

This chapter has been an examination of presidential midterm strategy, why it needs to be understood, what the literature has discovered already, and how we can get a better handle on it. Building off of the exiting literature, it has shown that there are valuable depths that research has yet to plumb, particularly in regard to the role of parties within midterm strategy. Taking my cue from the prior chapter, I have argued that presidential strategy is predicated not on simply electing as many partisans as possible, but of electing the rights ones, and that presidents take advantage of their increased partisan leeway to try and reshuffle their party (and the opposition) into something more closer resembling their own political beliefs.

The data show this to be true. Presidents are more likely to appear with, endorse, campaign for frequently, and campaign later in the year for a particular set of candidates—the needs of his party notwithstanding. These results, then, suggest a much different way of understanding presidential actions than has yet been put forward and a much different rational for what is occurring within midterm elections. The next step is applying these strategic findings to the outcomes of presidential actions and seeing whether presidential strategy is ultimately successful in (re)shaping American government. In the next chapter, then, I move beyond strategy to look at the impacts of presidential actions and show how presidents are (and are not) successful in their attempts to reshape the political and partisan environments in which they must act.

Notes

1. This again mirrors the prior chapter. The question of strategy in Chapter 4 was the method of engagement in campaigns—whether to continue to act behind the scenes or to embrace open involvement in the elections. This chapter builds on this by pushing the strategic choice one level lower into how that public campaigning is carried out.

2. As noted in Appendix A, the limitation in the data to post-1970 elections is due, in large part, to the problem of frequent redistricting and/or the creation and dissolution of at-large districts in the 1950s and 1960s.

3. This is, of course, high relative to presidential presence in the total universe of contested races but is rather shockingly low given that close contests ought to be particularly valuable "investments" from the presidential perspective.

4. "I'm delighted to see Christine Kehoe. And we are determined to see her prevail. If you want to do something for what you just stood up for, send her to Congress. Send her to Congress." William Jefferson Clinton, "Remarks at DNC Luncheon in Rancho Santa Fe, California (September 26, 1998)," in *Public Papers of the President of the United States: William Jefferson Clinton* (Washington, DC: U.S. Government Printing Office, 2000), p. 1679.

5. George W. Bush, "Remarks at a Luncheon for Representative Anne M. Winthrop in Louisville (September 5, 2002)," in *Public Papers of the President of the United States: George W. Bush* (Washington, DC: U.S. Government Printing Office, 2005), p. 1537.

6. Ibid.

7. Matthew Eshbaugh-Soha and Sean Nicholson-Crotty, "Presidential Campaigning in Midterm Elections," *American Review of Politics* 30, no. 1 (2009): 37.

8. Brendan J. Doherty, "'Elections': The Politics of the Permanent Campaign: Presidential Travel and the Electoral College, 1977–2004," *Presidential Studies Quarterly* 37, no. 4 (2007): 750—hereafter *Presidential Travel*.

9. Matthew Hoddie and Stephen Routh, "Predicting Presidential Presence: Explaining Presidential Midterm Elections Campaign Behavior," *Political Research Quarterly* 57: 257—hereafter *Presidential Presence*.

10. Patrick J. Sellers and Laura M. Denton, "Presidential Visits and Midterm Senate Elections," *Presidential Studies Quarterly* 36, no. 3 (2006): 450—hereafter *Presidential Visits*.

11. Doherty, *Presidential Travel*, p. 749.

12. Matthew Lang, Brandon Rottinghaus, and Gerhard Peters, "Polls and Elections: Revisiting Midterm Visits: Why the Type of Visit Matters," *Presidential Studies Quarterly* 41, no. 4 (2011): 809–18—hereafter *Revisiting Midterms*.

13. Sellers and Denton, *Presidential Visits*.

14. Lang et al., *Revisiting Midterms*.

15. Doherty, *Presidential Travel*.

16. Sellers and Denton, *Presidential Visits*.

17. Barbara Hinckley, "Interpreting House Midterm Elections. Toward a Measurement of the in-Party's 'Expected' Loss of Seats," *American Political Science Review* 61, no. 3 (1967): 691–700; Joseph E. Campbell, "Explaining Presidential Losses in Midterm Congressional Elections," *Journal of Politics* 47, no. 4 (1985): 1140–57; Bruce I. Oppenheimer, James A. Stimson, and Richard W. Waterman, "Interpreting U.S. Congressional Elections: The Exposure Thesis," *Legislative Studies Quarterly* 11, no. 2 (1986): 227–47.

18. Edward Tufte, "Determinants of the Outcomes of Midterm Congressional Elections," *American Political Science Review* 69, no. 3 (1975): 812–26; Richard

Born, "Strategic Politicians and Unresponsive Voters," *American Political Science Review* 80, no. 2 (1986): 599–612.

19. Kenneth Sheve and Michael Tomz, "Electoral Surprise and the Midterm Loss in U.S. Congressional Elections," *British Journal of Political Science* 29, no. 3 (1999): 507–21.

20. Walter Mebane and Jasjeet Sekhon, "Coordination and Policy Moderation at Midterm," *American Journal of Political Science* 96, no. 1 (2004): 392–411.

21. Robert Erikson, "The Puzzle of Midterm Loss Author," *Journal of Politics* 50, no. 4 (1988): 1011–29.

22. Campbell, *Seat Losses*, p. 181.

23. Joseph Campbell and Joe Sumners, "Presidential Coattails in Senate Elections," *American Political Science Review* 84, no. 2 (1990): 513–24; Gary Jacobson, "Presidential Coattails in 1972," *Public Opinion Quarterly* 40, no. 2 (1976): 194–200.

24. Charles Press, "Voting Statistics and Presidential Coattails," *American Political Science Review*, no. 4 (1958): 1041–50.

25. Gregory Flemming, "Presidential Coattails in Open-Seat Elections," *Legislative Studies Quarterly* 20, no. 2 (1995): 197–211; Russell Calvert and John Ferejohn, "Coattail Voting in Recent Presidential Elections," *American Political Science Review* 77, no. 2 (1983): 407–19; Herbert Kritzer and Robert Eubank, "Presidential Coattails Revisited: Partisanship and Incumbency Effects," *American Journal of Political Science* 23, no. 3 (1979): 615–26.

26. Paul Herrnson and Irwin Morris, "Presidential Campaigning in the 2002 Congressional Elections," *Legislative Studies Quarterly* 32, no. 4 (2007): 629–36.

27. Lang, *Revisiting Midterms*; Kelle et al., *2002 Congressional Elections*, p. 829.

28. Cohen et al., *Midterm Senate Elections*; Hoddie and Routh, *Presidential Presence*; Sellers and Denton, *Presidential Visits*.

29. Dustin McDaniel, "Presidential Midterm Campaign Strategy and Campaign Visits: The Case of 2002 and 2006," master's thesis, University of Georgia, Athens, GA, 2008; Lang, *Revisiting Midterms*; Eshbaugh-Soha and Sean Nicholson-Crotty, *Campaigning in Midterms*.

30. Eshbaugh-Soha and Nicholson–Crotty (2009), inter alia, document staffer statements about midterm strategy.

31. Sellers and Denton, *Presidential Visits*; Lang et al., *Revisiting Midterms*; Eshbaugh-Soha and Nicholson–Crotty, *Campaigning in Midterms*.

32. Kelle et al., *2002 Congressional Elections*, p. 829.

33. Doherty, *Presidential Travel*; Eshbaugh-Soha and Nicholson–Crotty, *Campaigning in Midterms*; Lang et al., *Revisiting Midterms*.

34. Lang, *Revisiting Midterms*, p. 810, Hoddie and Routh, *Presidential Presence*, p. 257.

35. Sellers and Denton, *Presidential Visits*, p. 412.

36. David Jackson, "Trump Says He'll Negotiate with Democrats on Health Care Plan," *USA Today*, September 27, 2017, https://www.usatoday.com/story/news/politics/2017/09/27/trump-says-hell-negotiate-democrats-health-care-plan/708790001/.

37. Dwight D. Eisenhower, "Address at the Hollywood Bowl, Los Angeles, California (September 23, 1954)," in *Public Papers of the President of the United States: Dwight D. Eisenhower* (Washington, DC: U.S. Government Printing Office, 1955), pp. 873–74.

38. Daniel Galvin, *Presidential Party Building: Dwight D. Eisenhower to George W. Bush* (Princeton, NJ: Princeton University Press, 2009).

39. "Extensive Nixon-Agnew Campaigns Have Mixed Results," *Congressional Quarterly Weekly Report*, November 6, 1970; this is the only time we see this type of behavior, though President Trump has threatened to do so in 2018.

40. Lou Cannon and Carl Cannon, *Reagan's Disciple: George W. Bush's Troubled Quest for a Presidential Legacy* (New York: Public Affairs, 2008), pp. 90–91.

CHAPTER SIX

The Impact of Presidential Midterm Campaigning

Presidents engage in midterm campaigning and have done so openly and without fear of punishment for the past 60 years. As the prior chapters have shown, this behavior is disruptive to the underlying relationship between the legislative and executive branches, and as such is a behavior that was once anathema to the political order. Yet, contemporary presidents campaign openly and actively because the forces that once stood in their way—namely, the American party system—have lost the internal capacity to resist presidential aggrandizement. They use these activities in an attempt to reshape the political environment in their own favor, by putting the resources of their office at the disposal of those candidates who are most favorable to them, ignoring even the needs of large portions of their own partisans. If the preceding chapters are correct, then these statements are true. But all of these actions are merely so much noise unless presidential midterm campaigning accomplishes a substantive outcome, unless it does actually allow presidents to reorder the political universe.

Yet, the evidence presented in the preceding chapters does not really show there to be any substantive impact from midterm campaigning—or at least not a positive one. The three "premodern" attempts of Johnson, Taft, and Roosevelt ended in disaster—impeachment, party schism, and end of domestic agenda, respectively. Certainly, presidents would not be so active in their midterm behaviors if they expected this outcome to occur. Likewise, midterm campaigning does not, at first blush, appear to functionally aid a president's partisan allies. This should be obvious from the fact the presidential party gets routinely walloped in midterm elections, with the only exceptions to this since the midterm campaign of 1954 being in 1998 and 2002—and the credit accorded to the political talents of Clinton and Bush (or their aides) might just as easily be given to the blistering, tech bubble–fueled economy, and the effects of previously unreached post-9/11 popularity. Thus, a cursory inspection of the history of midterm campaigning shows a heavy investment of presidential resources with very little obvious reward—and a great deal of trouble reaped instead.

But to stop at this "finding" and declare that midterm campaigning has no impact would be the height of academic arrogance, in that it would argue that real-world politicians have no actual understanding of how real politics works (and implicitly that the "Ivory Tower" understanding is superior). Moreover, this would imply that generations of presidents have needlessly wasted their time and energy on a useless pursuit. But maybe something else is going on that we simply do not see. The purpose of this chapter is to look at what else might be occurring and to show that midterm campaigning by presidents has a substantive and positive (from the presidential perspective) impact on American politics immediately, in the near future, and long term. There is no denying that midterm campaigning has an impact on American politics—it consumes a huge amount of presidential time—but if it does not have a subsequent impact, then it is a singularly odd behavior. The problem is that the existing scholarship has not found there to be any real impact; it has found that midterm campaigning singularly fails to move the needle. However, in a similar vein to the previous chapters, it is argued here that this is not because the existing scholarship is wrong—it is not—but rather that it takes too narrow of a view concerning what presidents might be after and what they receive for their efforts.

To show that midterm campaigning does have a meaningful impact on American politics, this chapter proceeds as follows. First, we look at the basic facts of midterm elections and how they do clearly suggest a limited return on the presidential investment. Moving past this, an understanding of existing scholarship is laid out, and it is shown why it is both entirely correct in interpreting the facts and unnecessarily shallow in the facts that it chooses to look at. Third, I lay out a new path of investigation that argues that midterm campaigning is only tangentially about the actual election and much more so about shaping the behavior of members of Congress and the voting public in subsequent years. Finally, I examine this by looking at the relationship between midterm campaigning and these behaviors, to show the important but overlooked impact of midterm campaigns.

The Problem of Midterm Campaigning

In the summer and fall of 2010, President Barack Obama found himself in a difficult situation. Facing an anemic economy (recovery summer!) and having gone through a brutal fight to pass the Affordable Care and Patient

Protection Act (Obamacare), his personal approval rating had fallen from a high of 64.63 in the afterglow of his inauguration to a low of 41.45,[1] and a new political opposition had arisen as "a platform for conservative popular discontent, [and] a force in Republican politics of revival"—the Tea Party.[2] Yet, even in the face of these dismal tidings, President Obama was adamant that the Republicans would not and could not regain control in Congress, telling the (Democratic) public:

> Imagine the economy's a car, and the Republicans drove it into a ditch. [*Laughter*] And it's a very steep ditch. So somehow the Republicans walked away from the scene of the accident . . . And we got to say, no. You can't have the keys back. You don't know how to drive. We can't give them the keys back.[3]

Moreover, the one-two punch of a re-energized opposition and crashing approval ratings never dampened his optimism about the ultimate outcome of the election and the importance of his role within it. When concerned Democrats asked him how they would be able to avoid a party-wide debacle such as had befallen them in 1994, he told them, "Well, the big difference between here and in '94 is you've got me."[4]

Still, President Obama did not simply trust to the fates (or the goodness of the electorate) and leave the outcome to chance. Rather, he undertook an aggressive campaign in waning months of the election season, traveling far and wide in support of Democratic candidates. He beseeched the American people to talk to their friends and "describe to them the future that you see for this country."[5] He reminded them that they had "the chance to set the direction not just for this State [*sic*], but for this country, for years to come."[6] He asked of them to "keep on believing . . . to talk to your neighbors . . . to go vote early."[7] He did so widely and broadly, campaigning for 114 candidates in 28 states and spending 56 days on the trail—a massive investment of time, energy, and effort. Yet, all of this was for naught, as the 2010 midterm was nothing short of a bloodbath for the Democratic Party, seeing it shed 63 seats (and the majority) in the House and six seats in the Senate. The new era of Democratic dominance that had seemed at hand only two years prior was gone, and President Obama was left with what he described as an "electoral 'shellacking' for his party."[8]

Mr. Obama was hardly the first president to be disappointed by the outcome of midterm elections. Since 1860, the presidential party has lost seats in the House in all but three elections—1934, 1998, and 2002. As noted in the previous chapters, the midterm loss is effectively the Old Faithful of American politics. It is not, as has also been made clear, for lack of trying by presidents; but try as they might, presidential efforts consistently fail to bear fruit. As Figure 6.1 makes clear, over the 20th century presidents greatly expanded

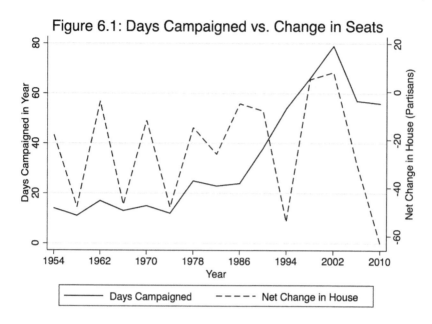

Figure 6.1: Days Campaigned vs. Change in Seats

their midterm campaigning. Unfortunately for presidents, there is no obvious correlation between campaign effort and campaign outcome, and indeed there is no clear indication that presidential efforts have fundamentally altered the outcome of midterm elections.

This is not to say that presidential campaigning does not, sometimes, appear to have important impacts. In 1998, for example, Bill Clinton was able to overcome the doom and gloom of talking heads who predicted veto-proof (and impeachment- and removal-enabling) Republican majorities in Congress—to pick up a handful of seats in the House (and rid himself of Newt Gingrich to boot).[9] Likewise, in 2002, George W. Bush was able to gain seats in the House and the Senate, gaining the majority in the latter while strengthening it in the former. Perhaps it is unsurprising then that these two midterms saw the highest ever levels of presidential campaigning and that these two men worked tirelessly to achieve these outcomes. Still, it is hard to overlook the fact that, their labors aside, Clinton had the benefit of an ineptly handled impeachment process and perhaps the greatest era of global economic prosperity in human history, and Bush was still gently sliding down from the political impact of 9/11—the highest presidential approval ratings of all time.

But for presidents bereft of these attributes, midterm campaigning appears to have been far from a good investment. From 1954 through 1994, virtually every president advanced on the efforts of their predecessor or their prior self, traveling more frequently and further, campaigning longer and harder. None appeared to be successful, and they also all lost seats in at least the House of Representatives. Moreover, there appears to be no connection between the level of investment and the subsequent return (or limit to the loss). President Eisenhower spent 17 days on the trail in 1954 and saw the loss of 18 seats in the House and two in the Senate; President Obama spent 56 days campaigning only to suffer far worse. Modern presidents have incredibly sophisticated and targeted methods, their analysis more advanced and their resources vastly superior.[10] Yet, with the rare exceptions of 1998 and 2002, presidents cannot claim a clearly definitive benefit from their actions. Given the immensity of the undertaking, the vast commitment of time and money, and the apparent presidential focus on this method of engagement, it behooves us to understand what it is that presidents get for their efforts.

Outcomes and the Literature

As noted in Chapter 4, the obvious thing to look for as the outcome of presidential midterm campaigning is the increased election (or increased vote share) of fellow partisans to Congress. Presidents, after all, spend this campaign time asking the people to please "elect," to "send money," to "help" certain candidates, and unless they construe the English language differently than the rest of us, it is clear that they do this with the hope of actually aiding these candidates' chances at the polls. Existing scholarship as well as anecdotal evidence tells us that campaigning is driven by the competitiveness of races and the popularity of presidents within tight areas, clearly with the intention of the getting the best possible return for their investment of time and resources.[11] Moreover, these are, after all, congressional elections, and presidential statements (as noted previously) are always directed at candidates and why their election is valuable. Thus, the idea that presidential campaigning seeks to elect ever more partisans is a most sensible place to start.

Although it is minimal, there is some evidence that midterm campaigning does help House and Senate candidates. Table 6.1 presents a simple model of midterm vote share for the House, broken down by visit type and drawing on three other factors: prior vote share, presidential popularity, and the six-month change in statewide unemployment. The results indicate that candidates do receive a significantly greater share of the two-party vote if they are graced by presidential attention—but that the greatest impact falls on those who receive the lightest presidential touch. Indeed, this model suggests an almost linear decrease in the impact of presidential actions as those actions scale up in terms of "effort," with a nearly 7 percent increase in vote share predicted from a simple appearance to a statistically (and substantively) insignificant amount for a fundraiser.[12] This could be a sign that "higher" levels of presidential activity have smaller impacts, or these actions accrue to

Table 6.1   **Predicting House Share by Campaign Type**

Variables	Visited	Endorsed	Fundraiser
Prior Share	0.83***	0.83***	0.83***
	(0.013)	(0.012)	(0.012)
Presidential Approval	0.27***	0.27***	0.28***
	(0.027)	(0.027)	(0.027)
Change in Unemployment	−1.35***	−1.05***	−1.08***
	(0.385)	(0.375)	(0.374)
Presence	6.80***	3.95***	0.39
	(0.832)	(1.051)	(1.940)
Constant	−9.95***	−9.33***	−9.65***
	(1.557)	(1.534)	(1.515)
Observations	3,546	3,752	3,792
Adj. R-squared	0.66	0.65	0.65

OLS regression; robust standard errors in parentheses.
*** $p < 0.01$, ** $p < 0.05$, * $p < 0.1$.

candidates in closer races and therefore are all the more consequential in spite of their "smaller" impact. Or they could signal that presidential efforts are misplaced and inconsequential.

Though it examines these elections in a different manner—odds of victory rather than vote share—similar results can be seen in Table 6.2, which models the probability of winning a given House seat at the midterm. As these results make clear, just as with its impact on the vote share, presidential campaign actions appear to have at best a light impact on a candidate's actual chances of victory or defeat. Although it is significant for simple presence, it is only weakly so when compared to other factors. More importantly, neither endorsements nor fundraisers are linked to a greater propensity to victory by affected candidates. Indeed, the sole consistent variable throughout that possesses any meaningful movement is presidential approval—suggesting that if a party won the seat previously and a president was relatively popular, the candidate has a high probability of winning the seat again, regardless of presidential actions. This, of course, makes sense and perhaps suggests a limited consequence for presidential campaign actions.[13]

The findings of these models fit well with the existing literature. Decades of research on presidential midterm campaigning have found little evidence that presidential actions have a substantive impact—either determining victory or defeat—on midterm election results. Presidential campaigning may impact the score (vote share), but it does not impact who wins the game. This is surprising, of course, given the emphasis that the literature places on

Table 6.2 Predicting House Outcomes by Campaign Type

Variables	Visited	Endorsed	Fundraiser
Won Previous	5.72***	5.79***	5.79***
	(0.180)	(0.180)	(0.177)
Presidential Approval	0.06***	0.06***	0.06***
	(0.007)	(0.007)	(0.007)
Change in Unemployment	−0.09	−0.08	−0.08
	(0.109)	(0.110)	(0.110)
Presence	0.48**	−0.08	−0.39
	(0.201)	(0.341)	(0.695)
Constant	−6.89***	−6.85***	−6.84***
	(0.449)	(0.443)	(0.442)
Observations	3,807	3,807	3,807
Pseudo R-squared	0.64	0.63	0.63

Logistic regression; robust standard errors in parentheses.

*** $p < 0.01$, ** $p < 0.05$, * $p < 0.1$.

midterm campaigning as being focused on electing or protecting partisan members of Congress. As we saw in the previous chapter, a sizable portion of the literature argues that the primary basis for presidential campaigning, the linchpin of midterm strategy, is to focus on close races because those are the races that presidents can help win. Presidents, we are told, focus their attention on "races where the clout of the president could make a difference."[14] They may grant more favor to those who support them more, and tailor their actions around things like popularity, but the goals of midterm actions are to elect these members in tight races.[15]

Yet, for all the energy the existing literature has put into arguing that the purpose of midterm campaigning is the election of more partisans, it has found almost zero evidence that this outcome occurs. Anecdotal evidence often hints at a strong presidential influence in this regard from campaign behavior, but at other times does not.[16] Cohen et al. (1991) find that although campaigned-for Senate candidates lost 65.6 percent of the time, most candidates fared better than those for whom the president did not campaign.[17] Likewise, Herrnson and Morris (2007) find that in the 2002 midterm elections, visits by President Bush significantly enhanced the prospects of campaigned-for candidates.[18] However, in direct opposition to this, Kelle et al. (2004) find that in the 2002 elections presidential activities had no discernable effects and that "future presidential attempts to influence congressional campaigns are not likely to be any more effective than in 2002."[19] Ragsdale (1980) finds similar outcomes in the 1970, 1974, and 1978, arguing that campaign activities are of limited importance and that non-presidential variables are the major predictors of the congressional vote.[20] In the end, some scholars find little, others almost nothing, and the rest zilch to support the idea that presidential campaigning impacts congressional elections.

In the face of this dearth of positive findings regarding the assumed purpose of midterm campaigning, one could decide to make another go of the same approach, to try to find some new and better way of examining the question with the same end in mind. But as much as that is the common way of doing this, it seems the wrong way forward, for two reasons. First, the sheer volume of time and ink that the literature has spent examining the extent to which midterm campaigning shapes election results, with no clear results itself, suggests that this is not simply a situation in which we are unable to *show* that presidential actions (within certain races) do alter the results of congressional elections. In fact, our inability to see a significant influence would make perfect sense as, given the presidential propensity to focus on close races, the races presidents spend their time on might very well break roughly 50/50 in the then-president's favor—making it practically impossible to tease out any significant pattern of presidential influence on the races themselves. It could be that we are missing some significant connection or explanation for the role of presidential campaigning, such that one is present but yet unaccounted for and unnoticed. Or it could be that presidential campaigning does not have a substantive impact on congressional elections; as Rasgdale (1980) suggests, congressional elections could simply be congressional, and not presidential, events.[21]

However, at a practical level the truth of the matter is much simpler: the extent to which presidential campaigning impacts congressional election is largely irrelevant. Understanding the impact of midterm campaigning through congressional returns may be empirically and theoretically satisfying, and the absence of concrete results may be puzzling, but to continue to focus on it obscures the simple truth that presidential campaigning continues to occur and consumes a significant and much increased portion of presidential time. We are thus left with two ways of understanding the situation. First, it could be that presidents and their staffs insist on continually expanding an undertaking that consumes immense presidential resources and publically links the president to (and against) vulnerable political actors, and that these astute politicos do so without finding some level of return commensurate to their efforts. Or we could broaden our gaze and accept that presidents might be receiving something from midterm campaigning that makes their efforts worthwhile, even if something is different from what scholarship has led us to believe. As it stands, we repeatedly try that same route and find the same dead ends. We could continue down this same path, but I suggest that the way forward is found in undertaking something rather different. That is what I propose to do.

New Interpretation of Presidential Campaigning

If the value of midterm campaigning is about more than the results of any given congressional election campaign, then what else could it be about? There are, of course, myriad possibilities, but I want to focus on two possible presidential goals that have been suggested so far by the discussion within the literature. First, even if they do not influence congressional election results, it is possible that presidential midterm campaigning impacts subsequent presidential results. Much of the literature suggests this to be the case, sensibly enough given its focus on the idea of midterm campaigning as an extension of the permanent campaign. Moreover, this thesis is not without real-world support, as presidential staffers have suggested this to be part of the presidential strategy within the campaign season. (This fits well with the theory examined in Chapter 4.) If presidential midterm campaigning is driven by intraparty and interparty instability (particularly at the state level), then it would make sense that such campaigning would be predicated on influencing state-level outcomes and, more importantly, state-level party institutions. For example, during the 2002 midterms, officials in the Bush administration explicitly linked their midterm efforts with Bush's chances of reelection, specifically noting the importance of state legislative and gubernatorial elections to Bush's chances in 2004.[22]

To be able to examine this possibility, we need to be able to place midterm campaigning within the context of presidential forecasting in order to understand how it impacts election results in relation to other, more well-studied factors. Unsurprisingly, the literature on presidential elections, voter choice, and forecasting is deep and varied, with multiple competing theories as to what drives voter behavior. At a fundamental level, however, debates in this area of research are rather simple, and they break down between those who see individual voters (and hence aggregate voter counts) as most concerned about economic outcomes and those who see them concerned with political performance.[23]

These two competing understandings, then, suggests divergent factors to look at when trying to understand or predict presidential election outcomes. Those who follow the economic line of thought tend to focus on proxies for economic health, be they gross domestic product (GDP) growth, income changes, or business confidence. There are numerous potential proxies, and it is more a matter of choosing one than on being able to do so. Some scholars use a "national business index"; others, a grouping of "leading economic indicators"; still others keep it simple and stick to per-capita income growth (and peace).[24] On the other hand, those who focus on "political" outcomes are largely left to focus on "national survey measures of "popularity," such as government satisfaction or presidential job approval."[25] Thus, these scholars are more limited in their tools but nonetheless use tools that are readily available.

Neither of these two camps suggests much of a role for presidential campaigning in the determination of presidential election results. Indeed, work by Finkel (1993) goes so far as to suggest that campaigning has no impact and that, at most, campaign actions activate voters rather than altering their vote choice.[26] However, the literature on midterm campaigning that is focused on the concept of the permanent campaign does argue that these actions are done with the intent to influence the outcome of subsequent voter behavior. How does this occur, if presidents are not "persuading" voters (albeit two years in advance)?

At its root, the impact of presidential midterm actions on subsequent presidential elections should come in the form of network activations. Presidential actions in various states should help to strengthen state and local party organizations, to increase the fervency of the mass-level supporters of the president's party, and (hopefully) increase that party's strength within state and local political units. Each of these is important, as each of these can have an impact in subsequent elections—state, congressional, and presidential. The strength of state and local parties, combined with the fervor of the local population, should make it all the easier to construct and maintain the necessary campaign infrastructure in state. Indeed, one of the great advantages of being an incumbent president is that having this infrastructure already in existence; midterm elections can certainly not harm this process and likely will help it.[27] Likewise, the election of fellow partisans to important state offices is just, if not more important. These officials help to ensure that presidential policies are enacted and favorably so, help to steer state and federal actions in the same manner, and are often quite effective campaigners for presidents (as Milbank [2002] suggested).[28] Just as importantly, midterm actions should give the incumbent party an advantage by establishing these networks before their future opponents are given the chance. Collectively, then, midterm actions have the potential to generate increased resources and support by creating or reactivating partisan and political networks in states.

In addition to impacting presidential, but not congressional, vote shares, I would suggest the possibility that presidential midterm actions impact congressional behavior, not congressional elections. As discussed in the previous chapter, the literature's focus on the election of partisans to Congress obscures the fact that what presidents should ultimately care about is how Congress behaves. Certainly they should want partisans in Congress, but that does not mean those partisans are particularly well aligned with presidential preferences. We saw outlines of this in the discussion of presidential strategy in the preceding chapter: presidential action was not merely predicated on the closeness of a given race, but also on the relative ideological placement of the candidates to the president. Put another way, presidential strategy is focused not simply on electing partisans, but on electing the *right* partisans— those most likely to aid and favor them. To bring this idea forward into the realm of potential campaign impacts, presidential goals should be based on returning a Congress that behaves as closely to his ideal ideological point as he can make them.

The obvious goal of this, then, is to return a Congress (at least within the president's party) that is most adapted to that president's personal ideal points and policy preferences. If the Congress is more ideologically aligned, then the policy that comes out will be closer to presidential preferences and will emerge at less political cost to presidents; so, all would be well. So, at its base, then, these actions are not about the mere election of partisan candidates, but about their behavior in the subsequent Congress. Modern presidents should not be partisan egoists who revel in the number of their allies they elect and the success of their party, but rather they should be personal egoists who revel in the number of personal policy goals they can achieve. Thus, the true aim of midterm campaigning should be to increase their overall levels of congressional support by winning future favors from these "favored" members.

This brings midterm behaviors into the realm of congressional decision-making. This literature suggests two competing understandings of congressional motivations. First, it looks at them from the perspective of Congress as an institution. Key to this is the work of Adler and Lipinski (1997).[29] They, with others, argue on behalf of strong, demand-side committees that direct the work of the larger body, with logrolling occurring between the committees to get favored projects completed. Alongside this is the work of Shepsle and Weingast (1987), who add in a notion of a committee ex post veto, through which legislation is ultimately controlled by the originating committee via the conference bill.[30] A third line of argument often taken is on behalf of (conditional) party governance. Put forward by Rohde (1991), this argues that parties, given certain factors, can organize their chamber in such a fashion as to completely control it, ensuring that leadership decisions are almost invariably followed.[31] Seconding these findings are Aldrich and Rohde (1998), Cox and McCubbins (2007), and Smith (2007), who all find pervasive effects from the organizational actions of parties.[32] Fourth and finally, there is the notion of ideology as the determining factor in congressional behavior. This is most strongly argued by Krehbiel (1991/1993/1998), who holds out that parties are rather irrelevant factors in that their influence cannot be discerned past the exercise of basic ideological behavior.[33] Hence, in this world the Congress is simply a body of ideological individuals, and party effects are simply the echoes of the innate, ideological choices that would already be made.

A second body of literature has examined the linkages that exist between executive actions/pressures/wishes and congressional behaviors. For presidents, these linkages are of supreme importance as every president has a legislative program, and key to their success is simply "getting his most important proposals on the congressional agenda."[34] In determining what factors are the are most important, scholars have discovered something of a mixed bag. Bond and Fleisher (1990) argue for a number of possibilities ranging from policy domain to the prowess and makeup of the congressional leadership.[35] However, they find evidence that party and ideology are far more influential at ensuring success than more presidentially based factors such as popularity or legislative skill.[36] Likewise, Edwards and Barrett (2000) find that presidential advantages at agenda setting are limited to times of unified government, and dissipate when strict partisanship comes to the fore. Finally, Edwards (1989) finds that both "congressional party cohorts and public support are the principle underpinnings of presidential leadership of Congress," but he makes clear that these resources are interdependent: one without the other is almost meaningless.[37]

However, only one set of scholars has examined the relationship between midterm campaigning and congressional voting. Herrnson, Morris, and McTague (2011) look at the 1998 and 2002 midterms and find evidence that presidential campaigning did cause members of the president's party to increase their levels of support for presidential policies.[38] Although they lay a solid foundation, and I plan to extend their use of campaign frequency as the key variable, I want to expand on their effort in two major ways. First, I want to introduce campaign timing into the analysis. As we saw in the last chapter, timing matters in terms of strategy. I argue that this arises because timing changes the value of presidential visits; as such, that changing calculus should be reflected in changing congressional behavior, and those candidates who receive campaign aid in the waning days of the cycle should be more receptive (and more obligated) to helping push through the president's proposals.

Though Herrnson et al. (2011) eschew looking at this, I suspect the opposite behavior is true as well—that is, members of the opposition who are campaigned against should react negatively to presidential actions, and become less favorable to presidential policies.[39] This fits the strategy seen in the preceding chapter. As we saw, presidential midterm strategy is not simply focused on partisans, but on opponents, with presidents more likely to campaign against ideologically distant members of the opposition. In addition to merely wanting them defeated, presidents should also favor campaigning against them because any potential blowback (and blowback should occur) will be limited given that these individuals are highly unlikely to support much of the president's agenda anyway. Thus, just as I presume that midterm campaigning will increase support for the president's agenda among partisans as a function of frequency and timing, and I believe it will decrease it among members of the opposition.

Analysis and Results

Let us examine if these presumptions are correct, starting first with the impact of modern campaigning on subsequent presidential elections. Table 6.3 shows a simple model of presidential vote share from 1976–2008. It looks at

Table 6.3 Predicted Vote Share in State

Variables	Model
Won Prior	0.70***
	(0.050)
Presidential Approval	0.17***
	(0.030)
Change in Unemployment	0.32
	(0.539)
Total Days	0.74***
	(0.173)
Constant	3.92
	(2.669)
Observations	450
Adjusted R-squared	0.54

OLS regression; robust standard errors in parentheses.
*** $p < 0.01$, ** $p < 0.05$, * $p < 0.1$.

four factors: the share of the two-party vote won by the incumbent president's party in the previous election, presidential popularity on Election Day, the change in state-level unemployment over the six months preceding Election Day, and the total number of days the president spent in that state during the midterm cycle. Though the model is simple, it is designed to capture a base level of support (prior election), a national indicator (popularity), a state-level indicator (unemployment), and a presidential action (total days).

The results of the model indicate that midterm campaigning has a small but significant impact on subsequent presidential elections—roughly a 0.7 percent increase in the two-party vote share per day spent in the state. This is not a huge impact, but it could be an important one. Figures 6.2 and 6.3 display the deciding states in the 2000 and 2004 presidential elections, with the actual two-party share for the party of the incumbent president and the portion of that share this model attributes to midterm campaigning. As you can see, this model argues that one of the reasons Gore lost in 2000 and Bush won in 2004 was because of the method of campaigning in the preceding midterm cycle. In both 1998 and 2002, Presidents Clinton and Bush hit the trail as if their lives depended on it, but they handled their campaigns in very different fashions. President Clinton focused his attention on a series of large fundraising events in major (Democratic-leaning) cities in Texas, California, and Illinois. This raised colossal sums for the party but did not necessarily connect with voters in key states. President Bush spread his actions

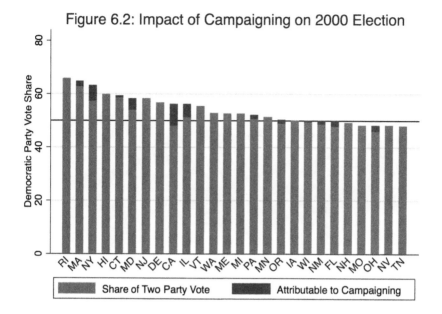

Figure 6.2: Impact of Campaigning on 2000 Election

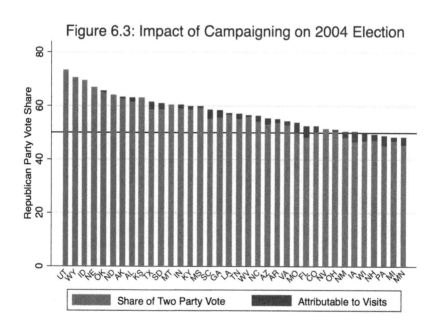

Figure 6.3: Impact of Campaigning on 2004 Election

across a much wider range of states and focused his attention on individual races and candidates—connection much more at the local level. Consequently, it is quite possible that the reason we had two terms of Bush instead (of at least one) of Gore is because George Bush used his midterm travel far more strategically than did Bill Clinton.

Something similar can be seen if you examine this through a logistic model of state-level win/loss. The results of such a model are presented in Table 6.4 and are remarkably like those in the vote share model. Both suggest an important role for midterm campaigning, but this model puts it into clearer context. As it shows, midterm campaigning does impact the likelihood of winning a state, with a substitution rate of about 4–1 between presidential popularity and presidential campaign attention; thus, a day of campaigning has the statistical influence of four points on the presidential approval score. It is important, but not overwhelmingly so.

The nature of this influence is further shown in Figure 6.4, which shows the marginal effect of campaigning across levels of popularity. As it shows, the impact of midterm campaigning is different depending on the strength of a president's popularity and the nature of the state in question. Moreover, it suggests that midterm campaigning can be thought of as a defensive weapon—it serves to beef up the party in states that the party already wins. While the impact of presidential campaigning in states a president did not win increases

Table 6.4　Probability of Winning State

Variables	Model
Won Prior	3.44***
	(0.364)
Presidential Approval	0.06***
	(0.014)
Change in Unemployment	0.06
	(0.245)
Total Days	0.23**
	(0.102)
Constant	−5.59***
	(0.768)
Observations	450
Pseudo R-squared	0.32

Logistic Regression; Robust standard errors in parentheses.

*** $p < 0.01$, ** $p < 0.05$, * $p < 0.1$.

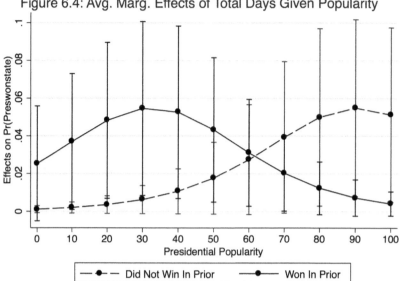

Figure 6.4: Avg. Marg. Effects of Total Days Given Popularity

greatly as popularity increases (with a mirrored fall in states that have already been won), this shows mostly a theoretical state as no president has gone into a presidential election with much greater than 60 percent approval.

Collectively, these two models support the idea that midterm campaigning impacts subsequent presidential elections. Midterm campaigning influences subsequent outcomes (or at least helps explain them), but in a potentially defensive fashion; presidents do not benefit from midterm campaigning by gaining support in new states, but by preserving their prior levels of support in states they had previously won. Indeed, the only election in which midterm campaigning appears to have determined the winner is 2004, when 50 electoral votes won by President Bush came in states where his campaigning may have provided the margin (Florida, Iowa, Missouri, and New Mexico); perhaps, more than just congressional majorities stood in the balance in the fall of 2002. It may be a limited impact, but it is a substantive one.

The second potential impact of midterm campaigning that we need to examine is the extent to which campaign actions impact subsequent congressional behavior. The idea is that midterm actions are part of quid pro quo— the president scratches Congress's back, and its members scratch his in return. As such, presidential midterm actions should create a debt or vendetta among members of Congress, and this is repaid in the subsequent session by increased or decreased support for the president's agenda.

To examine this, we need to look at congressional voting behavior, specifically levels of support for the president's legislative agenda. Table 6.5 shows

Table 6.5   Impact of Campaigning on Senate Support Scores

Variables	Returning Partisans	All Partisans	Returning Opponents	All Opponents
Prior Support	0.67***		0.35***	
	(0.052)		(0.049)	
Presidential Approval	0.12**	0.26***	−0.16***	0.07
	(0.051)	(0.057)	(0.050)	(0.050)
Ideological Distance	−13.84***	−30.05***	−20.76***	−29.25***
	(3.420)	(3.592)	(2.762)	(2.823)
Presidential Influence	0.02	−0.01	0.04	0.02
	(0.038)	(0.048)	(0.047)	(0.043)
Days Campaigned	−0.02	2.21**	−0.85	0.22
	(1.004)	(0.897)	(0.857)	(0.932)
Constant	18.80***	69.87***	50.90***	62.71***
	(4.557)	(2.755)	(3.935)	(3.669)
Observations	487	530	472	544
Adjusted R-squared	0.37	0.15	0.28	0.21

OLS regression; robust standard errors in parentheses.

*** $p < 0.01$, ** $p < 0.05$, * $p < 0.1$

the results of a model looking at presidential support in the Senate from 1970 to 2010. It finds support for the idea that midterm campaigning alters congressional voting behavior, but only when looking at all senators—thus losing the ability to take prior levels of support into account. However, it does suggest that midterm campaigning can have a significant impact for partisan senators. As the table shows, each day of campaigning increases presidential support by roughly 2 percent. This may not seem like a great deal, but the median partisan senator supports the president approximately 75 percent of the time—so each day of campaigning gobbles up roughly 10 percent of all remaining possible support. It may be limited to a subset of senators, but it still has a significant impact.

These findings are seconded by the results of the model looking at voting behavior in the House, the results of which are presented in Table 6.6. These results clearly indicate both a substantive impact from midterm campaigning and an impact that is moderated by parties. There is a significant impact on presidential support across all four categories of representatives, and—as predicted—there is a significant negative response for members of the opposition party. Thus, the major difference between these results and those for the Senate is that they show a stronger distinction in the reaction by partisans and opponents—changes in behavior are much more pronounced, depending on the party of the impacted member. This makes sense, as the House is traditionally the more majoritarian and partisan chamber. This, then, suggests yet another reason why presidents ought to be as thoughtful and strategic as possible in how they organize their midterm campaigns.

Collectively, these findings suggest two important things. First, they affirm the literature's focus on midterm campaigning as an aspect of the permanent campaign. Presidential actions in the midterm elections do appear to directly influence outcomes in the subsequent presidential elections, causing a small but potentially impactful increase in support for the president or his party's candidate. I argue that this occurs because midterm campaigning helps to activate and develop networks of support in various states, which then aid and advantage presidents within their own reelection attempts. Midterm campaigning serves to prime the pump, so to speak, by developing networks on behalf of others that can then be used for a president's own advantage.

Second, and more importantly, these findings indicate a new way of understanding midterm campaigning's impact on congressional behavior. While Herrnson et al. have shown previously that midterm actions alter congressional voting behavior, these results extend and expand them.[40] For one, they push the analysis onto a broader time frame and show that it is applicable across eras. This pulls forward the findings of the preceding chapter to show that not only do presidents strategically schedule their midterm campaigns but that these strategic choices have varied impacts. Thus, presidents are right to be strategic in how they deploy these midterm events, and we have another wrinkle of presidential–congressional relations to understand

Discussion and Conclusion

In the fall of 2010, President Barack Obama and his allies in Congress were "shellacked." The once proud White House had been laid low, and the Republicans were resurgent. However, this was not for lack of trying on the part of the president. Yet, for all his efforts, for all his fundraising, and for all his travel, he found himself in this situation. In this, Mr. Obama was in a similar position to all but two of his predecessors in midterm campaigns—on the losing side. We are left to wonder what all those thousands of miles and days of travel got them if, in the end, they all landed in the same (defeated) position.

The purpose of this chapter has been to examine this question and to suggest new possible answers. The existing literature is fixated on the notion that the expected impact of presidential midterm campaigns is to be found in increased midterm victories. Unfortunately, evidence of this has proven, as a

Table 6.6　Campaign Impact on House Support Scores

Variables	Returning Partisans	All Partisans	Returning Opponents	All Opponents
Prior Support	0.42***		0.15***	
	(0.022)		(0.028)	
Presidential Approval	0.13***	0.19***	0.13***	0.13***
	(0.029)	(0.033)	(0.023)	(0.023)
Ideological Distance	−12.57***	−29.51***	−21.94***	−23.72***
	(2.018)	(2.002)	(1.961)	(1.326)
Presidential Influence	0.15***	0.14***	0.01	0.01
	(0.025)	(0.028)	(0.015)	(0.015)
Days Campaigned	1.62***	3.32***	−4.12***	−4.16***
	(0.472)	(0.525)	(1.065)	(0.951)
Constant	42.40***	75.30***	35.65***	40.62***
	(2.165)	(1.799)	(3.034)	(1.869)
Observations	1,974	2,080	2,367	2,567
Adjusted R-squared	0.42	0.24	0.30	0.21

Robust standard errors in parentheses.

*** $p < 0.01$, ** $p < 0.05$, * $p < 0.1$.

unicorn, elusive to find. Consequently, I suggested two different outcomes—increased support from Congress and increased voter support in the presidential election—as the true potential outcomes of midterm campaigning. After analyzing midterm campaigning in relation to both subsequent presidential elections and congressional voting behavior, it looks clear that there is strong evidence to support for both hypotheses.

Although it is validating to find that presidential midterm actions do, indeed, increase electoral strength in the following presidential election, it is not entirely remarkable. This is an idea that is firmly lodged within the literature; these analyses, far from reshaping those thoughts, merely confirmed and extended it. What is remarkable and important, however, are the findings regarding congressional voting behavior, which provide a significant extension of our understanding.

However, what is important is that this impact exists at all, that though presidents may not cause more of their partisans to be elected, they still reap significant rewards for their undertakings. It hints, in an interesting way, that presidents are stacking the deck—that even before the Congress comes into session, before all the intricacies of congressional decision-making are brought to bear, some level of advantage has already been gained. This suggests the potential for a major revision in our understanding of how Congress behaves, how presidents interact with Congress, and how our institutions are structured to be responsive to the public rather than to each other. Thus, they are at least not insignificant findings.

Indeed, these findings combined with those of the previous two chapters suggest a major revision of our understanding of what the place, purpose, and impact of midterm campaigning is, and what that means for American politics. Our institutional and partisan structures were designed for a purpose, to deal with a set of expectations; presidential midterm campaigning exists and acts in such a manner as to dramatically upend them. In the next chapter, I tie together these three threads of midterm campaigning and examine what they suggest about the future.

Notes

1. Polling data were retrieved at various points in the fall of 2012 from The Gallup Brain: Presidential Job Approval Center. These data are available (with subscription) from http://news.gallup.com/interactives/185273/presidential-job -approval-center.aspx.

2. David Barstow, "Tea Party Lights Fuse for Rebellion on Right," *New York Times*, February 15, 2010, p. A1.

3. "Remarks at a Democratic National Committee Rally in Bridgeport, Connecticut (October 20, 2010)," in *Public Papers of the President of the United States: Barack H. Obama (2010)* (Washington, DC: U.S. Government Printing Office, 2013), p. 3—hereafter "Bridgeport, CT."

4. Glenn Thrush, "Berry: Obama Said 'Big Difference' between '10 and '94 Is 'Me,'" *Politico*, January 25, 2010, http://www.politico.com/blogs/glennthrush/0110 /Berry_Obama_said_big_difference_between_10_and_94_is_me.html.

5. Barack H. Obama, "Remarks at a Democratic National Committee Rally in Philadelphia, Pennsylvania (October 20, 2010)," in *Public Papers of the President of the United States: Barack H. Obama (2010)* (Washington, DC: U.S. Government Printing Office, 2013), p. 2.

6. Obama, "Bridgeport, CT," p. 1.

7. "Remarks at Democratic National Committee Rally in Cleveland, Ohio (October 31, 2010)," in *Public Papers of the President of the United States: Barack H. Obama (2010)* (Washington, DC: U.S. Government Printing Office, 2013), p. 7.

8. Peter Baker and Carl Hulse, "Deep Rifts Divide Obama and Republicans," *New York Times*, November 3, 2010, p. A1.

9. Nancy Gibbs and Michael Duffy, "Fall of the House of Newt," CNN -Allpoliitcs.com. November 16, 1998, http://www.cnn.com/ALLPOLITICS/time /1998/11/09/gingrich.html.

10. An excellent examination of modern campaign strategy—including specific methods such as micro-targeting—can be found in Michael Burton, William

Miller, and Daniel Shea, *Campaign Craft: The Strategies, Tactics, and Art of Political Campaign Management* (Santa Barbara, CA: Praeger, 2015).

11. Jeffrey E. Cohen, Michael A. Krassa, and John A. Hamman, "The Impact of Presidential Campaigning on Midterm U.S. Senate Elections," *American Political Science Review* 85, no. 1 (1991): 166–78; Matthew Hoddie and Stephen Routh, "Predicting Presidential Presence: Explaining Presidential Midterm Elections Campaign Behavior," *Political Research Quarterly* 57, no. 2 (2004): 257–65.

12. An "appearance" simply refers to a candidate being at the same public event as the president and being recognized. See Appendix A for greater information on the coding schema and method.

13. This also helps explain the outcomes of the 1998 and 2002 midterm elections, in which Presidents Clinton and Bush had Gallop approval ratings of 65 and 67 percent, respectively, 90 days out from the midterm—the two highest ratings at that point in the data set.

14. Luke Kelle, Brian Fogarty, and James Stimson, "Presidential Campaigning in the 2002 Congressional Elections," *PS: Political Science and Politics* 37, no. 4 (2004): 829.

15. McDaniel, Campaign Visits; Hoddie and Routh, "Predicting Presidential Presence"; Patrick J. Sellers and Laura M. Denton, "Presidential Visits and Midterm Senate Elections," *Presidential Studies Quarterly* 36, no. 3 (2006): 410–32.

16. "Extensive Nixon-Agnew Campaigns Have Mixed Results," *Congressional Quarterly Weekly Report*, November 6, 1970; Kelle et al., "2002 Congressional Elections"; "Ford's Election Impact," *Congressional Quarterly Weekly Report*, November 9, 1974; "Another Stubborn Democratic Congress," *Congressional Quarterly Weekly Report*, November 4, 1978.

17. Cohen et al., "Midterm Senate Elections," p. 166.

18. Paul Herrnson and Irwin Morris, "Presidential Campaigning in the 2002 Congressional Elections," *Legislative Studies Quarterly* 32, no.4 (2007): 629–48.

19. Kelle et al., "2002 Congressional Elections," p. 832.

20. Lyn Ragsdale, "The Fiction of Congressional Elections as Presidential Events," *British Journal of Political Science* 8, no. 4 (1980): 375–98.

21. Ibid.

22. Mike Allen, "For Bush, the Stump Goes On: 8th Trip to Iowa Highlights Focus on the Key States for 2002, '04," *Washington Post*, November 9, 2002, p. A04; Dana Milbank, "The Virtual Candidate: Bush Could Win or Lose for Next Two Years on Nov. 5," *Washington Post*, November 2, 2002, p. A01.

23. Michael Lewis-Beck and Charles Tien, "Election Forecasting: Theory, Practice, Japan," American Political Science Association 2011 Annual Meeting paper, revised August 14, 2011, http://papers.ssrn.com/sol3/papers.cfm?abstract_id =1902848.

24. Michael Lewis-Beck and Charles Tien, "Election Forecasting for Turbulent Times," *PS: Political Science and Politics* 45, no. 4 (2012): 625–29; Robert Erikson and Christopher Wiezein, "The Objective and Subjective Economy and the Presidential Vote," *PS: Political Science and Politics* 45, no. 4 (2012): 620–24;

Douglas A. Hibbs Jr., "Obama's Reelection Prospects under 'Bread and Peace' Voting in the 2012 Presidential Election," *PS: Political Science and Politics* 45, no. 4 (2012): 635–39.

25. Lewis-Beck and Tien, "Theory, Practice, Japan."

26. Steven Finkel, "Reexamining the 'Minimal Effects' Model in Recent Presidential Campaigns," *Journal of Politics* 55, no. 1 (1993): 1–21.

27. Tim Dickinson, "No We Can't," *Rolling Stone*, February 2, 2010, http://www.rollingstone.com/politics/news/no-we-cant-20100202.

28. Milbank, "Virtual Candidate."

29. Scott E. Alder and John S. Lipinski, "Demand-Side Theory and Congressional Committee Composition," *American Journal of Political Science* 41, no. 3 (1997): 895–918.

30. Kenneth Shepsle and Barry Weingast, "Institutional Foundations of Committee Power," *American Journal of Political Science* 81, no. 1 (1987): 85–104.

31. David Rhode, *Parties and Leaders in the Post-Reform House* (Chicago: University of Chicago Press, 1991).

32. John Aldrich and David Rohde, "The Transition to Republican Rule in the House: Implications for Theories of Congressional Politics," *Political Science Quarterly* 112, no. 4 (1998): 541–67; Gary Cox and Matthew McCubbins, *Legislative Leviathan: Party Government in the House* (Cambridge, MA: Cambridge University Press, 2007); Steven Smith, *Party Influence in Congress* (Cambridge: Cambridge University Press, 2007).

33. Keith Krehbiel, *Information and Legislative Organization* (Ann Arbor: University of Michigan Press, 1991); Keith Krehbiel, "Where's the Party?," *British Journal of Political Science* 23, no. 2 (1993): 235–66; Keith Krehbiel, *Pivotal Politics* (Chicago: University of Chicago Press, 1998).

34. George C. Edwards III and Andrew Barrett, "Presidential Agenda Setting in Congress," in Jon R. Bond and Richard Fleisher (eds.), *Polarized Politics* (Washington, DC: CQ Press, 2000), p. 110.

35. Ibid.

36. Jon R. Bond and Richard Fleischer, *The President in the Legislative Arena* (Chicago: University of Chicago Press, 1990), p. 222.

37. George C. Edwards III, *At the Margins: Presidential Leadership of Congress* (New Haven, CT: Yale University Press, 1989), p. 217.

38. Herrnson, Paul, Morris Irwin, and William McTague, "The Impact of Presidential Campaigning for Congress on Presidential Support in the U.S. House of Representative," *Legislative Studies Quarterly* 36, no. 1 (2011): 99–122.

39. Ibid.

40. Ibid.

CHAPTER SEVEN

The Future of Midterm Campaigning

"So, I think, while I recognize the limitations of Presidential campaigning, traditionally it has not been very successful, at least I think it may arouse some interest in this campaign and encourage the turnout . . . So, if we can arouse some interest and cause a bigger turnout then I'll feel I've done the job, even though history's against us."[1]

In the autumn of 1954, President Dwight D. Eisenhower threw down a gauntlet and broke a long-standing political taboo by actively and publically campaigning within that year's midterm congressional elections. Rather than seeing these actions resented and rejected by political elites—as had happened to his predecessors who had engaged in similar actions—Ike's campaign was accepted with passive indifference. Moreover, rather than being a one-off undertaking, midterm campaigning became part of the normal suite of presidential actions. The modest beginnings of the Eisenhower White House were built on by Jack Kennedy, who engaged in a wide-ranging and vigorous campaign that would set the template for subsequent decades. Presidents Nixon and Reagan added their mark by instilling an emphasis on Senate campaigns and by deliberately focusing their efforts on the future growth of their party and the importance of their roles in trying to expand their parties into new areas.[2] The 1990s and 2000s saw these efforts continued, and saw Bill Clinton and the two Presidents Bush investing huge amounts of time raising funds, not for candidates but for the party as an institution, cementing the importance of the president to the party rather than the reverse. Indeed, each president that followed Eisenhower took up midterm campaigning, adding his own foci but also acting to build up the received behavior. But what about the future?

As was shown by the preceding chapters, midterm campaigning is a (relatively) new arrival to our political scene and a behavior that arose in reaction to a changed political and partisan world. As such, it has allowed presidents to channel resources and assistance to chosen candidates, to try and get (re)elected those men and women whom they most favor. Yet, while the evidence in Chapter 6 is quite convincing that presidential campaigning does influence congressional voting behavior and has marginal impacts on subsequent presidential elections, there is no obvious evidence that midterm campaigns have resulted in landslides for the presidential party, for major reshuffling of the makeup or behavior of Congress, or for major legislative accomplishments. The Civil Rights Act was not passed because of Kennedy's efforts in 1962; the Reagan Revolution floundered in spite of Reagan's (then) herculean efforts in 1982 and 1986; and even seemingly successful attempts (such as Clinton's in 1998 and Bush's in 2002) can largely be chalked up to non-campaign-related forces—and had no obvious impact of presidential policy making.[3] Consequently, it would seem perfectly reasonable for presidents and their aides to heed the wisdom of the existing literature and call time on the experiment that is midterm campaigning. It would be logical to do so, given how little presidents have to show in the way of tangible benefit for all the time and effort that have been spent on midterm campaigning in the past 60-odd years.

Yet, taking this line of reasoning would (as noted previously) require us to assume that we in the academy are correct, and those in the world of practical politics are wrong. If we approach it from the perspective of the arena rather than the ivory tower, everything about the political situation suggests that midterm campaigning—far from dwindling—will only deepen as a presidential behavior going forward. But this raises the question: If, in the face of apparent failure, midterm campaigning is to continue and to expand or deepen, how will it look and how will it impact the political order?

The task of this chapter is to briefly examine the future state of midterm campaigning and its importance to the American polity. To do this, the chapter proceeds in two directions. First, I examine the potential actions of President Donald Trump in the upcoming 2018 midterm contest. Drawing on the political situation that exists one year into his term, as well as the from the findings of the prior chapters, I offer a discussion of the potential shape of his campaign and how well it accords (or does not fit) with the received behavior of his predecessors. Second, I discuss the long-term impacts of this behavior and what it means for our understanding of American politics. I close by arguing that our current perceptions of the place of midterm campaigning are wrong and that it follows a long-held pattern of failing to see the import of changes and an overestimation of our political system's ability to easily react to underlying change.

In 2018 and Beyond

The 2018 midterm and the Trump presidency are the perfect jumping-off point for a discussion of the future and importance of midterm campaigning. On one hand, this is because the 2018 cycle will likely be make or break for the Trump White House. We need only look to history to see that if the Republicans maintain control over Capitol Hill, they stand a decent chance of maintaining the White House in 2020; if they are routed, then those chances fall dramatically. Consequently, given the stakes of the election and the personality of this particular chief executive, I think we can expect a very particular approach to the midterms from the White House. Namely, we should see a president who does not campaign as his immediate predecessors have done—that is, those post WWII—but rather one who approaches the midterm as an opportunity for transformational change within the party (system) and therefore behaves more aggressively vis-à-vis his party than we have seen in the postwar era. This leads to the more important reason why the 2018 election is a good place to start: the situation in which Donald Trump finds himself in the winter of 2017–18 is eerily like his premodern predecessors.

First, all three of the premodern attempts at presidential midterm campaigning found their genesis in the utter collapse of the presidential legislative agenda at the hands of Congress. For Andrew Johnson, the overriding legislative goal was the full readmittance of the Southern states and the restoration of the prewar Union—on presidential terms. This agenda died at the hands of the rump Congress, particularly in the fights over Johnson's vetoes of the Freedman's Bureau and civil rights legislation. In the case of Taft, the hope was simply to carry out the platform on which he was elected— moderately progressive and yet not antithetical to the Old Guard. These hopes vanished in the "compromise" that was tariff revision and in the fights over Speaker Cannon. Likewise, FDR believed that his second term would herald the second New Deal—less a series of emergency measures than a fundamental reordering of the political and economic environment. Unfortunately, the Wages and Hours Bill, the Executive Reorganization Bill, and the Court Packing Plan all went down in flames—alongside judicial actions that picked apart actions of his first term.

Second, each of these presidents traced their legislative failures to the structure of their party within Congress—specifically, to the factional divisions of those parties. For Johnson, the ascendency of the Radicals within the Republican Party hindered his ability to govern with a "union coalition"—moderate Republicans and War Democrats working to restore the Union to, effectively, status quo antebellum, with acceptance of the end of slavery. Taft's troubles were with the liberal Progressive wing of the Republican Party and their ongoing feud with the Old Guard, which hindered any united actions. With Franklin Roosevelt, the problems were geographic, with the more conservative (and traditionally foundational) Southern wing of the Democratic Party increasingly at odds with the ever more liberal Northern faction. In each case, the failure of the president's policy agenda was not a function of the opposition, but rather of the unwillingness of some portion of his own party to work with him.[4]

Third, each president believed that the way out of the political quagmire he found himself in was not further compromise with the dissident elements of his own party, but rather through his cleansing and the subsequent strengthening of the more favorable faction. Thus, Andrew Johnson focused his efforts on the destruction of the Ben Wades and the Thaddeus Stevenses of the Republican Party in order to strengthen the more conservative faction that would in turn be able to work with moderate Democrats to advance his agenda. President Taft faced an exclusively Republican situation, favoring the support of the Old Guard/standpats and their ascendency within the party through the defeat of the Progressive wing. Likewise, FDR concentrated his energy on purging the Democratic Party of its conservative elements in order to rebuild the Party into a new, president-oriented, liberal force.

Thus, the first year of the presidency of Donald Trump is, in many respects, a 21st-century retelling of these three prior cases. On the legislative side, the new president has seen his agenda slow down, completely halt, and then catch on fire. The attempts of the White House and the Republican Congress to "repeal and replace" the Patient Protection and Affordable Care Act have failed on two separate occasions and appear to have ceased for the time being.[5] The call to "build the wall" has gone nowhere, as Congress has shown itself unwilling to fund the project in the absence of the unexpected failure by Mexico to do so.[6] Finally, although eventually making its way through Congress, the "tax reform" bill that made its way to Trump's desk in December of 2017 bore little resemblance to the proposals of the Trump Administration or of senior Republican figures—though they are no doubt pleased to have gotten half a loaf.[7] Thus, virtually the entire legislative agenda on which President Trump ran in 2016 is in danger of repudiation or collapse.

Importantly, these failures occurred with a substantial Republican majority in the House of Representatives and a Republican majority in the Senate more than capable of passing important legislation (Repeal and Replace) through the reconciliation process, thus bypassing the possibility of a Democratic filibuster. Thus, the collapse of the Trump legislative agenda is a function of internal divisions of the Republican Party just as clearly as the split within the Democrats caused the failures of the Roosevelt administration in 1937–38. The ideological distance between the Tea Party/Freedom Caucus faction and the "establishment" Republicans in many ways mirrors that of the Progressives and the Old Guard, and thwarts any major policy proposals by negating the on-paper Republican majority through internecine strife.

Thus, one year into his presidency, President Trump finds himself in a remarkably similar position to Presidents Taft and Roosevelt—seemingly politically adrift due, in no small part, to an inability to work with the constraints of the partisan order (even when that order has gifted him congressional majority). This presents the obvious possibility that in the 2018 election Mr. Trump will not be emulating his postwar predecessors in engaging in midterm campaigning. They did so with the goal of changing their party—certainly—but they did so understanding that they were constrained by that party and their actions had to be necessarily circumscribed. Does that circumspection necessarily exist in the Trump White House?

Indeed, it seems that such behavior is not in the cards with the Trump administration. Rather, at least with regard to the subject of midterm campaigning, it appears quite proper to join the inexorable chorus of the Huffington Post and MSNBC, and call President Donald Trump a monster. However, while his opponents hurl it as a derogatory word, I would suggest it in the original Latin sense of the term—a monster (*monstrum*) was something that warned humanity, an omen. For better or worse, there is no denying that the Trump presidency is a warning in some regard, as he represents the epitome of the modern, public presidency. He combines the characteristics of the archetypal demagogue with the sensibilities of the modern TV entertainer, wrapping them together in a package that is revolting or inspiring, intriguing or depressing, depending on one's perspective. He represents the logical end of the path the presidency has been traveling for generations, a warning of what that means—and a warning as to how midterm campaigning can be used in such hands.

As such, President Trump is both the embodiment of the mercenary president under whom midterm campaigning should attain its purest expression, and a president who may prove so unconcerned with the behavior as to render it temporarily moot. This is because on one hand the midterm campaigns of the past 60 years have been examples of planning and discipline—as the preceding chapters have shown, presidents strategically picked out places and races in which to campaign, and deliberately acted and spoke in ways to draw attention (and favor) to the candidates best suited to adding their causes.[8] While the Trump campaign of 2016 could be held up as a model of strategic planning, it could also be easily argued that the president lacks the discipline necessary to carry off a yearlong set of actions on behalf of other persons—particularly given that he appeared to have very little in the way of coattails in his general election campaign. At the same time, the Trump presidency also shows us the pure example of a president driven by ego, of a mercenary presidency for which party has little meaningful attachment. Consequently, Donald Trump ought to be the perfect president to engage in the ruthless form of midterm campaigning suggested in Chapter 5, wherein a president seeks not to elect the largest number of partisans, but rather seeks to return the Congress most amenable to his own desires—regardless of the impact of such actions on the president's nominal party.

President Trump fits this concept to a tee, in part because he is clearly an atypical president when it comes to partisanship. While Dwight Eisenhower is frequently suggested as being only moderately partisan, and Herbert Hoover was actually floated as a candidate on a bi-partisan "Liberal" ticket, Donald Trump can easily be considered the least partisan president of the last 100 years, and probably since the Grant administration (if not further).[9] This should not be surprising given that Mr. Trump has not only been rather loose in his party affiliation, but has given large sums of money to both current congressional opponents and the opponent be bested for the office he currently holds.[10] Therefore, it would surprising if President Trump did not have the urge to cross party lines and establish a working majority consisting of the most ideologically proximate members of the House and Senate. Indeed, he has already tacitly proposed doing so, going out of his way to attack the most conservative blocks of the Republican Party while making overtures to members of the Democratic Party in order to secure support for legislative goals.[11] Policy over party.

This tendency to eschew partisanship and party goals in favor of presidential ego is likewise reflected in President Trump's tendency to publically threaten members of his own party, even going so far as to suggest supporting primary challengers. The most vocal attacks have been against Congressman Mark Sanford (SC) and Senator Jeff Flake (AZ). Representative Sanford refused to back the "repeal and replace" efforts with regards to the Affordable Care Act. According to media reports the White House made it clear that the cost for such behavior would be open support of a primary opponent by the Trump administration.[12] In a similar vein, after having trouble dealing with Senator Flake on a series of issues, Mr. Trump held meeting with several individuals who have suggested running against him for state party nomination in 2018—an internecine fight that culminated in a public rebuke of the President by Mr. Flake, and a contemporaneous announcement of the Senator's retirement from Congress.[13] These actions by President Trump are nearly unprecedented in the post-WWII political world, with only Richard Nixon ever campaigning against a sitting member of his own party. Yet, it is not surprising—midterm campaigning is so ingrained, and partisan defenses against it so weakened, that there appears little threat of a party-wide reaction like in 1910 or 1938. Since there is no fear, why should the president not reshape the party in his own image?

However, unlike many of his predecessors in the postwar era, President Trump lacks the political capital necessary to reshape his party "politely." That is to say, from Eisenhower to Obama (with the exception of Nixon), presidents may have favored certain elements within their own party, but they never actively attacked their own members. Rather, they focused the destructive energy of the campaign on the opposing party, singling out vulnerable representatives and senators to try to defeat. However, as Chapter 5 made clear, this is largely a function of potential influence—popularity and coattails. There is little reason to suspect that President Trump will have substantive coattails in the 2018 cycle, effectively precluding worthwhile campaigning in enemy territory. Rather, it seems likely that he will have to limit his efforts to districts and states that are already solidly Republican, forsaking the opportunity to turn what might have been winnable seats in a number of states.

If President Trump is limited to campaigning in races for seats already held by the party, that undoubtedly changes when and how he campaigns. Most importantly, it should push his campaigning away from the general elections and toward the primaries, and away from the public rally and toward the private fundraiser. This push toward the primary season we can already see—his constant spats with and threats against members such as Sanford and Flake, along with his active participation in the 2017 Alabama special election primary, already place Trump in a class of his own when it comes to internecine squabbling via midterm campaigning.[14] Moreover, although he showed limited proclivity for fundraising in the 2016 presidential cycle, the facts on the ground ought to make that his most favored activity in 2018, much like it was with Presidents Clinton and Bush in 1998 and 2006. Moreover, these fundraising activities will allow President Trump potentially greater sway over the future of the party, as he will control more of the financial leverage than he otherwise would. Consequently, Trump's behavior should represent an amalgam of modern second-term presidents—who tend to focus on party-building activities because of their lower public standing—and pre-Eisenhower attempts to use midterm campaigning as a tool to out and out batter the party into submission. Indeed, this is perhaps what a second Nixon midterm campaign would have looked like, had he escaped/survived Watergate (and possessed Twitter), rather than the second-term campaigns that we have gotten used to; the president may have a weaker capacity to reshape the party, but he will possess one nonetheless.

Moreover, we should not expect this "deepening" midterm campaigning to be confined to the Trump administration and the 2018 cycle alone. Rather, the political environment as a whole suggests a number of reasons why we should expect this as a standard facet of future presidential behavior. For one, it appears that the presidency is increasingly narcissistic. It is no stretch of the imagination to label Donald Trump in the literal (tragic) sense.[15] Any number of things—from his inability to avoid Twitter spats to his tendency to describe all things related to himself, his businesses, or his administration as "the best"—speak to his rather inflated sense of self.[16] This is not to impugn his character or deny his claims—I leave that to others to debate—but rather merely an observation about the state of the presidency in 2017. Moreover, it would be impolite to suggest that he is alone in this character trait among politicians, or among recent presidents. Indeed, one need only look to the example of his predecessors to see an individual with an equally high level of self-regard—let us not forget the personal seal of the presidency created during the 2008 campaign; *Vero possumus*, indeed.[17] This narcissism should both fuel the desire for deeper involvement in midterm (and all congressional) campaigns and also mentally insulate the president from any pushback due to this behavior or failures within the campaign.

Likewise, the apparently increasing populism of the American electorate should further fuel presidential involvement. At a basic level, higher levels of populism ought to simply make it harder for the parties to control the public, the flip side of this being that this ought to create even more avenues for presidential involvement. As noted above, presidents became increasingly active in midterm campaigning in the 1970s and 1980s in part because of the dealignment of voters from parties, which in turn fueled further candidate independence and more opportunities (and requirements) of presidential involvement. Although the increasing populism of the electorate—the Tea Party-ish movements in the Republican Party and the Occupy Wall Street/ Bernie Bro movements on the Democratic side—have been largely contained within the two major parties, it nevertheless weakens the ability of the two parties to control the electoral process, again fueling desires for presidential involvement.

Collectively, then, we ought to see an increased level (in tenor if not in number) of presidential involvement in midterm campaigns until the political situation stabilizes. The United States appears, in 2017, to be operating in an extended period of what Skowronek would call "the politics of disjunction."[18] The incomplete nature of the Reagan Revolution combined with the apparent failure of 2008 as a realigning election has left the United States in a political lurch. For the past 30-some years—and since the turn of the 21st century— we have seen the two parties throw a series of political haymakers at each other, and none of them seem to have landed—one party seems ascendant only to be quickly dashed by the opposition. This has led to an unsettled situation in which neither party is dominant, and so no party acts as the sun to the other's moon. This disjuncture creates the environment in which midterm campaigning can grow because the actors that might be able to stand in the way lack the obvious backing to do so. Thus, not only are the types of person likely to become president increasingly orientated to the types of behavior required for a more dangerous form of midterm campaigning, and the electorate more inclined to allow it, but the political system as a whole is less capable of restraining it.

Why This Matters

These predictions may prove incorrect, but they are not the sum importance of this book. Rather, the value of this project is found more in the extent to which it reshapes how we think of and approach midterm campaigning than how we quantify and analyze it. This goal of this project is not to declare the modes and methods that have come before it to be wrong; rather, it has been an attempt to show that if we look up from the assigned path of inquiry, if we expand our field of view, then we can see and understand this behavior and its importance in ways that suggest whole new manners of exploration. As such, it has suggested three major points that we as scholars should ponder as we consider presidential midterm campaigning, congressional-executive relationships, and American politics broadly.

The first of these takeaway points is the importance of understanding the nature of presidential agency as a driving force in presidential behavior. Much of the literature looking at midterm campaigning and the modern presidency allows itself to be caught up in the narrative of modernity as a distinct thing, and of the public presidency and the permanent campaign representing new presidential ambitions rather than new modes of action. Thus, presidential actions are reduced to either somewhat irrelevant subunits of important global trends or of outcomes that in some ways must occur—modernity demands it. As I suggested at the outset of this book, this understanding is deeply problematic. This is not to say that midterm campaigning is not an important feature of the public presidency or of the permanent campaign; far from it, as it is clearly an integral and expanding part of both. But it is not an outcome determined by these larger trends; rather, it is an independent action that helped to bring these trends into full bloom.

Indeed, the single most important point of this whole book might be this: presidents did not have to involve themselves in midterm campaigns in the manner that they do, nor did they have to expand their efforts to the extent that they have. A world without midterm campaigning would be much different, and perhaps the power of the presidency would be less than it is currently, but the republic would have survived, and the presidency would no doubt be at least *primum inter pars* within the American political universe. That midterm campaigning does exist, then, and that it has expanded to the extent that it has, is not a function of something preconditioned, but rather the direct result of a series of presidential choices. Midterm campaigning arose as a rational response to a changed and changing political environment; its expansion was an equally rational response to a similarly changing environment. Its existence is not predetermined, and it is not necessary—it was a choice like any other, deliberately made.

This element of choice is all the more important to highlight because it is so often overlooked within the literature. By focusing on it, by placing presidential actions within the universe of possible alternatives, we are able to see presidential midterm campaigning in a whole new light. Not only can its rise and growth be better understood, but so too its organization and its expectations. As we saw in Chapter 5, by understanding midterm campaigning as a series of choices, we can more fully understand that presidential strategy really is presidential in nature—that the behavior exists to serve the president, not the candidate. This is a dramatic break from the conception of midterm campaigning as partisan service aimed at protecting vulnerable partisans; in its place, we can see presidents as strategic actors, making use of their campaign time to aid and indebt the members of Congress who will be most useful to their causes.

A second takeaway point from this book is the overarching importance of the party system within any proper understanding of American politics. As this book showed, whether as the patronage-driven, mass-public forms of the 19th century; the lost in the wilderness, fallen giants of the mid 20th century; or the renewed and reinvigorated service-orientated parties of now, parties structure and delineate the acceptable behaviors of American politics. Midterm campaigning was one such behavior, once treated as anathema, but now largely accepted. Unfortunately, the existing literature places no role for party in its vision of the behavior, no place for the structure and reward/punishment that the party system can provide. But as we saw, the party system is the key to the whole undertaking. It was changes in the party system that allowed midterm campaigning to realistically occur, that allowed presidential agency to take center stage.

This is important because it stresses the need for both those who look at midterm campaigning and those who look at American parties to understand the interplay that brought this behavior about and the ways in which party continues to define and be defined by it. For it is a two-way street. On one hand, modern presidents are clearly bent on dominating the party system and bending it to their will. As Milkis and Rhodes (2007) point out, recent presidencies—most well defined in the tenure of George W. Bush—have sought to remake their parties into presidential parties, to make their congressional counterparts not equals, but pure allies.[19] Midterm campaigning clearly plays a role in this, as we saw above. By allowing presidents to campaign for their favored candidates, they allow a virtuous/vicious (depending on your point of view) cycle to develop, wherein candidates receive and exchange aid and punishment with the president, wholly outside of the party structure. Midterm campaigning helps to accelerate the ability of presidents to "capture their parties"; this in turn is a function of the quiescence of the two parties, and that could vanish in the face of heavy-handed treatment.

Third, the findings of the preceding chapters make clear the importance of understanding the nature of the American party system and the way that its structure shapes the political universe in which it exists. Party is, of course, key to understanding midterm campaigning, as it defines the limits of acceptable behavior and constitutes the easiest means of punishing unacceptable behavior. The agency that presidents can now show within midterm campaigning is thus a function of a transformed party system: once such behavior was restricted or forbidden; now it is not, so it is freely and openly practiced. Likewise, the manner in which midterm campaigning is practiced is also a function of the party system. The attempts of Johnson, Taft, and Roosevelt failed because they occurred in the face of a partisan order built and determined to resist presidential encroachment; to the extent that modern attempts succeed, it is because they face a different pattern of resistance and encouragement.

Beyond this, the state of parties is all the more important as it not only structures the manner in which presidents can campaign but how those campaigns are received by Congress, the ways they alter how presidents interact with the institution, and how Congress actually behaves. Indeed, unless we take a strictly intuitionalist tack and argue for a sole focus on committees[20] or look only at constituency factors, the party ultimately defines this relationship. Parties, though acting differently than they once did, still organize and structure the Congress,[21] and if a president cannot translate popular support into partisan support, then it is meaningless.[22] However, even more explicit ideas of party—like the notion of "conditional party government"—obscure the true importance of party by overlooking the fact that it matters who in this relationship calls the shots: the party or the president.[23]

This, then, is the reason that party is quintessentially implicated in midterm campaigning—not only does it "cause" it to occur, but it is potentially radically altered by that occurrence. As Milkis and Rhodes (2007) point out, the modern presidency is focused on not simply assuming leadership of their party, but in subsuming the party in its entirety.[24] This is not a new desire—as Woodrow Wilson (1908) stated: "His patronage touches every community in the United States. He can often by its use disconnect and even master the local managers of his own party by combining the arts of the politician with the duties of the statesmen, and he can go far towards establishing a complete personal domination."[25]

But midterm campaigning provides something new. It is certainly part of a larger presidential strategy—Galvin (2010) shows at length how presidents have acted in the last 60 years to strengthen their parties, on their own terms; midterm campaigning is part of this.[26] But what sets midterm campaigning—or any of these actions—apart from prior actions like the use of patronage is that they appear to be nothing out of the ordinary, and yet are; they appear to be structured to aid the party, when they are structured to aid the president. This is not something to be lightly overlooked.

Ultimately, then, what this makes clear is the importance of understanding political changes in a systemic context, of understanding how a transformation of one aspect relates to the whole. Presidential midterm campaigning is, on its face, a minor change in our political system, an extension of long-established and accepted presidential actions. It is, in many ways, simply a facet of the public presidency, of the permanent campaign, of things that both the public and the political order accept without question or complaint: it ought to be small and insignificant. However, in its operation and in its impact, it is more than this, because of how midterm campaigning fits with the overall political system. As we have seen, midterm campaigning is an assault on a traditional order, a threat to an established (though changing) party system and the relationships its structures. To simply accept presidential midterm campaigning (and similar manifestations of presidential behavior) as par for the course, and just how it is, is to ignore the radical difference and potential change it represents. These behaviors represent a square peg that we, as scholars, simply assume fits into a round hole; that may not be the case.

By simply accepting this behavior and treating it as just another development, scholars understate its importance and overlook the extent to which it challenges long-held assumptions of American politics. Midterm campaigning does not simply threaten an established partisan system, but it represents a presidential attempt to undermine fundamental tenets of our political order. Our notions of representation and of the separation of powers, which come to us from the Founders on down, are predicated on the idea that ambition can counteract ambition, that pride of place will be something of value and will consequently animate political action. But whether these have ultimately proved effective (and they seem rather to have not), the extent to which they can depends on ensuring that the legislative and executive branches meet each other within government, that the manner in which they partner or fight be one developed between elected officials, not one decided prior to election. Presidential midterm campaigning threatens this system and upends notions of the separation of powers because it short-circuits process and establishes loyalty or enmity, presidential strength or weakness prior to the time when representatives or senators can meet the president as constitutional equals. Pride of place is unlikely to trump senses of debt or obligation, nor will ambition counteract ambition very often if it involves biting the hand that feeds—necessity will triumph, in the end. Presidential midterm campaigning may not be better or worse than that which has come before—be it patronage or outright graft—but it serves a similar purpose, and we do wrong to overlook that significance.

This is not meant to be a jeremiad against presidential campaigning or a reactionary statement that the old order must be preserved and this "menace" put down; far from it. Presidential midterm campaigning and all it represents is neither good nor bad in itself, and the impacts it has on our political system are certainly not normatively problematic. But this is a behavior that is potentially destabilizing to our established understanding of how American politics works—and we do not really have a backup model. If a president can gain an advantage even through what is perceived as a failure; if he is able to steer resources to fellow party members not on the basis of need (or worth), but on the basis of his own desires; if presidents can be successful in reshaping Congress and congressional behavior in their own image, then that is something worth understanding. Presidents seek mastery—that is in the nature of their office, and nothing new. But the institutions we have developed are, at least in theory, designed to channel that motive, to blunt it, to control it. If that is no longer the case; if midterm campaigning and actions like it allow presidents power and control through and within the institutions that are supposed to blunt them, then we need to understand how and to what extent that occurs. That this should come to be is neither good nor bad in and of itself; but it may be bad (and harmful) if we do not see it occurring and if we simply assume that square pegs will fit into round holes.

Notes

1. "John F. Kennedy, "Transcript of Interview with William Lawrence, recorded for the program 'Politics—'62' (October 14, 1962)," in *Public Papers of the President of the United States: John F. Kennedy (1962)* (Washington, DC: U.S. Government Printing Office, 1963), p. 777.

2. For Nixon, the 1970 campaign was part and parcel of the Southern strategy, an effort that was furthered—though in different fashions—under the Reagan White House. See, for example, Daniel Galvin, *Presidential Party Building: Dwight D. Eisenhower to George W. Bush* (Princeton: Princeton University Press, 2010), p. 20—hereafter *Party Building*.

3. This is not, however, to discount the extent to which these elections might have impacted non-policy outcomes. For example, if the Republicans had won more of the close Senate races that year—such as Wisconsin and Nevada, which both came within 1 percent—they might not only have had the wind at their sails for the upcoming impeachment fight, but they might have had the numbers to pull it off. Likewise, the 2002 elections certainly aided President Bush's subsequent invasion of Iraq (which likely would have occurred either way) but, more importantly, helped ensure that Republicans held sufficient votes to later appoint Justices Roberts and Alito.

4. Granted, in the case of Johnson he was effectively a Democrat elected on the Republican ticket, but there is little point in denying that the Union Party of 1864 was merely a thin veneer placed over the otherwise Republican administration.

5. The drive to repeal the Affordable Care Act was at the heart of the Trump "100-Day" agenda—it did not succeed. M. J. Lee, Lauren Fox, and Tami Luhby, "Donald Trump's Rude Awakening," CNN, April 27, 2017, http://www.cnn.com /2017/04/27/politics/donald-trump-health-care-100-days/index.html.

6. Z. Byron Wolf, "For Trump's Wall, Mexico Is Out! Government Shutdown Is In!," CNN, August 23, 2017, http://www.cnn.com/2017/08/23/politics/trump -wall-mexico-government-shutdown/index.html. The plan to build the wall not only stalled in late 2017 but ran into the immovable object that is Cards Against Humanity. Ginger Rough, "'Cards Against Humanity' wants to stop Trump's border wall," *USA Today*, November 15, 2017, https://www.usatoday.com/story/news

/politics/onpolitics/2017/11/15/cards-against-humanity-trump-border-wall
/865187001/.

7. Stephen Collinson, "Tax Passage Will Be a Moment of Vindication for
Ryan," CNN, December 20, 2017, http://www.cnn.com/2017/12/20/politics/tax
-reform-republicans-paul-ryan/index.html.

8. Frank Donatelli, "Trump and the GOP Need Message Discipline," RealClear
Politics, June 8, 2016, https://www.realclearpolitics.com/articles/2016/06/08/trump
_and_the_gop_need_ message_discipline_130818.html; Charles Blow, "Donald Trump's Lack of Discipline and Discernment," *New York Times*, October 27, 2016,
https://www.nytimes.com/2016/10/27/opinion/campaign-stops/donald-trumps
-lack-of-discipline-and-discernment.html; Dana Bash, "Can Teleprompter Trump
Stay Disciplined?," CNN, November 3, 2016, http://www.cnn.com/2016/11/03
/politics/donald-trump-2016-election-campaign-discipline/index.html.

9. In the run-up to the 1920 election a "liberal" ticket was floated that would
have consisted of Herbert Hoover (who had helped manage international food
aid during the First World War) for president and Assistant Secretary of the Navy
Franklin Roosevelt as vice president. See David Pietrusza, *1920: The Year of Six
Presidents* (New York: Basic Books, 2007).

10. This is not only a common behavior for President Trump but also for major
players in his administration. Phillip Bump, "If Donations to Democrats Mean
You're Anti-Trump, the White House Is in Very Deep Trouble," *Washington Post*,
July 24, 2017, https://www.washingtonpost.com/news/politics/wp/2017/07/24/if
-donations-to-democrats-mean-youre-anti-trump-the-white-house-is-in-very
-deep-trouble/?utm_term=.363ac55353ee.

11. Mary Kay Linge, "Trump Taunts GOP with Possible Health Care Deal with
Dems," *New York Post*, October 7, 2017, http://nypost.com/2017/10/07/trump
-taunts-gop-with-possible-health-care-deal-with-dems/; Donald Trump, "I Called
Chuck Schumer Yesterday to See If the Dems Want to Do a Great HealthCare
Bill . . . ," *Twitter*, October 7, 2017, https://twitter.com/realDonaldTrump/status
/916638685914951680.

12. Tim Alberta, "I'm a Dead Man Walking," *Politico*, February 17, 2017, https://
www.politico.com/magazine/story/2017/02/mark-sanford-profile-214791; Eliza Col-
lins, "Report: Trump Threatened Sanford with Primary If He Voted against Obam
acare Repeal," *USA Today*, March 30, 2017, https://www.usatoday.com/story/news
/politics/onpolitics/2017/03/30/report-trump-threatened-sanford-primary-if-he
-voted-against-repeal/99834866/.

13. Alex Isenstadt, "Trump Met with Potential Flake Challengers before Phoe-
nix Rally," *Politico*, August 23, 2017, https://www.politico.com/story/2017/08/23
/trump-jeff-flake-arizona-senate-241959; Alex Isenstadt and Kevin Robillard,
"Flake Announces Retirement as He Denounces Trump," *Politico*, October 24, 2017,
https://www.politico.com/story /2017/10/24/flake-retiring-after-2018-244114.

14. In the 2017 Alabama special election, the Trump administration curiously
followed the lead of the Republican Senatorial Campaign Committee (RSCC)
and backed Luther Strange over Roy Moore—odd, as Moore was backed by the

"Trump" elements within the party. Phillip Bump, "Trump Backs the Non-Trumpian Candidate in a Place That Likes Trump," *Washington Post*, September 18, 2017, https://www.washingtonpost.com/news/politics/wp/2017/09/18/trump-backs -the-non-trump-like-candidate-in-a-place-that-likes-trumps/?utm_term= .603e36d38a12. Moreover, in this race President Trump also showed the power of modern technology to hide earlier statements. Russell Goldman, "Trump Deletes Tweets Supporting Luther Strange," *New York Times*, September 27, 2017, https:// www.nytimes.com/2017/09/27/us/politics/trump-deletes-tweets.html.

15. Narcissus, of course, fell in love with his own reflection and continued to stare at it until he died. Although the story is Greek in origin, the standard version of this tale comes out of Ovid's *Metamorphoses*, Book III, ed. William Anderson, (Norman, OK: University of Oklahoma Press, 1997).

16. Chris Cillizza, "Donald Trump Ranked Himself Second on the List of Most "Presidential" Presidents," CNN, June 26, 2017, http://www.cnn.com/2017/07/26 /politics/donald-trump-abe-lincoln/index.html. In President Trump's defense, his predecessor did suggest (midway through his first term) that he was the fourth best president of all time; Steve Croft, "Interview with President Obama," *60 Minutes*, December 11, 2011, https://www.cbsnews.com/news/interview-with-president-obama-the-full-transcript/.

17. John Broder, "The Great Seal of Obamaland?," *New York Times*, June 20, 2008, https://thecaucus.blogs.nytimes.com/2008/06/20/the-great-seal-of-obamaland/.

18. Steven Skowronek, *The Politics Presidents Make: Leadership from John Adams to Bill Clinton* (Cambridge, MA: Cambridge University Press, 1997).

19. Sydney M. Milkis, and Jesse H. Rhodes, "George W. Bush, the Republican Party, and the 'New' American Party System," *Perspectives on Politics* 5, no. 3 (2007)—hereafter *New Party System*.

20. Kenneth Shepsle and Barry Weingast, "Institutional Foundations of Committee Power," *American Political Science Review* 81, no. 1 (1987): 85–104; Scott E. Adler and John S. Lapinski, "Demand-Side Theory and Congressional Committee Composition," *American Journal of Political Science* 41, no. 3 (1997): 895–918.

21. John H. Aldrich and David W. Rohde. "The Transition to Republican Rule in the House: Implications for Theories of Congressional Politics," *Political Science Quarterly* 112, no. 4 (1998): 541–67; Gary Cox and Matthew McCubbins, *Legislative Leviathan: Party Government in the House* (Cambridge, MA: Cambridge University Press, 2007); Steven Smith, *Party Influence in Congress* (Cambridge: Cambridge University Press, 2007).

22. George C. Edwards III, *At the Margins: Presidential Leadership of Congress* (New Haven, CT: Yale University Press, 1989).

23. David Rhode, *Parties and Leaders in the Post-Reform House* (Chicago: University of Chicago Press, 1991).

24. Sydney M. Milkis, and Jesse H. Rhodes, *New Party System*.

25. Woodrow Wilson, *Constitutional Government in the United States* (New York: Columbia University Press, 1908), p. 215.

26. Galvin, *Presidential Party Building*.

Midterm Data Set

The heart of the empirical side of this analysis is the midterm data set. This data set was constructed in order to capture every public campaign utterance in a midterm year from 1954 to 2010. It was compiled through an examination of the presidential statements contained in the public papers of the president. Although the data are available for public inspection and duplication at MichaelJulius.net, herein are described the way the papers were parsed and the data coded, to make it clearer what was and was not captured, and why.

When to Include: Timing

The first factor in determining the scope of the data set was to decide what years would be included in the analysis. Originally, all midterm years from 1954–2010 were included. Each was put through paces listed herein, and all relevant information tabulated. However, after looking over these data, it became clear that only the data from 1970 onward was of particular use—at least at the House level. This is primarily because of the fights over civil rights and redistricting in the 1950s and 1960s. These led to frequent changes not only in the shape of districts but also the types of election—state switching between at-large and district seats. These changes made it impossible for the data prior to 1970 to be made comparable to the data after 1970 and also made it hard to make use of important data, such as presidential vote share in each district, in a useful way.

After deciding what years to include, the next decision was how to determine the "campaign year." This is, on many levels, a completely arbitrary decision. There is no methodological reason to limit the examination to one year (or a fraction thereof) rather than the entirety of the period between the presidential election and the midterm. Likewise, there is no objective reason that determines how long that fraction of a year should be. Moreover, the choice of the "campaign year" is obviously tremendously important, as the window of observation used by the data determines its result. Thus, for good or ill, the midterm campaign season (for the purpose of this project) extends between New Year's Day and Election Day in each midterm election year—a maximum of 310 days and a minimum of 304.[1]

The choice of this as the window was driven by two main factors. First, there was no good reason to go to back beyond the start of the calendar year. The only logical period significantly longer than this would have been an examination of the entire two-year cycle, and that would have required an exorbitant amount of labor for rather small returns; presidents tend to be frugal in their campaigning, and it is highly focused within the calendar year of the midterm. Likewise, extending it back to be a full year—November to November—would have likely see almost no purchase, as presidents are not heavy (campaign) travelers during the holiday season. Consequently, it made no sense to encompass a larger window of time than January to November of each midterm year.

Second, it made no sense to go smaller than that either. Although the "traditional" campaign season was Labor Day and forward, presidential midterm campaigning moved beyond this (significantly) by the late 1970s. Although the bulk of the travel tends to be found in the second half of the year, many presidents were active in the early months, particularly in more recent years. Thus, there was no happy medium in the middle of the year that would satisfy both the value of brevity and the need for inclusion of as much travel as possible. As a result, January 1 was as logical a start date as any, and no substantive benefit appears to be possible from standardizing the number of days examined in each year.

What to Include: Events

After deciding what calendar dates to include, the next decision was to determine which events were worthy of inclusion. As noted above, all presidential events in the New Year's Day to Election Day window were examined and parsed; the set was intended to capture the entire universe of campaigning, not a random sample. However, this does not mean that all events were examined with the same level of thoroughness. Rather, a three-step process was used to filter and sort the events into appropriate silos.

First, events were examined to determine whether they constituted campaign travel. Events were classified as non-campaign if they were (1) nonpolitical, (2) nonpartisan, or (3) leadership only. "Nonpolitical" events were generally things such as commencements or commissionings, at which presidents routinely failed to make any sort of political (i.e., campaign-related) speech. For example, a common presidential event is the inspection of federal facilities. Frequently presidents visit these places and make statements, but their statements are banal observations about policy rather than politics.

"Nonpartisan" events were those at which members of the opposition party were present and recognized by the president; no president in this sample was brazen enough to copy FDR's example and endorse one candidate while the other sat next to him. Finally, "leadership-only" events were those at which either the Republican or Democratic leaderships were present—generally party retreats—but no outside actors were present. Thus, although presidents made many political statements at these events, they were never really directed at particular candidates or, more importantly, at the public.

Next, campaign events were subdivided into public and private. Public events were either those listed overtly as being a "rally," or when they were "Remarks at City/School/Business" and that particular place was somewhere where political speech occurred. Private events were those listed as fundraisers, lunches, dinners, and receptions (or some variation of those terms). The distinction between these was not necessarily the number of people— it is entirely possible that there were more people at many of these private events (large fundraisers) than there were at many of the public events (remarks at a business)—but rather the access afforded to the public and the media in disseminating the president's comments. Public events were those at which there was a high likelihood of media presence and therefore wide-scale distribution of the statements made; private events were those at which there was little to no likelihood of those statements being made widely public. Thus, in the former the audience was the mass public, and in the latter the audience was elites. Both types of events have value, but they ought to have different value from the presidential and the candidate perspective.

Finally, these events were also broken down on the basis of whom they were for—local elite, national elite, or personal. Local elite events were those that were private but were held for local political units—state or local parties, being the obvious example. National elite events were also private, but these were held for the national political units—the Republican National Convention (RNC) or the Democratic Congressional Campaign Committee (DCCC), for example. The distinction here was about audience. From a resource perspective, the distinction might be irrelevant, but from a campaign impact perspective it ought to matter more if a candidate is talked up in the place he or she is running (local elite) rather than at a party gathering in a random city (national elite). Finally, personal events were those listed as being on behalf of a particular candidate. These took the form of both public (rally) and private (fundraiser) events and should show the highest level of presidential commitment as they are done on behalf of a single candidate.

How to Include It: Coding

After deciding which events were included and which of those were worth exploration, the final (and most important step) was to content-analyze each and every statement. The potential presidential statements were both written and spoken; written statements were not included in this analysis as they either did not involve campaigning or were press releases and "summations" of upcoming speeches.[2] The spoken statements can be further subdivided into official pronouncements, pressers, and campaign/travel speech. Official pronouncements—such as bill signings or international speeches—were wholly excluded from the analysis, as were statements to the press/interviews. Ultimately, then, the only portions of the *Papers* that were included in the analysis were speeches made by presidents in private events that included some level of candidate endorsement (or were specifically labeled as fund-raisers) and public events that mentioned partisan candidates and at which members of the opposing party were present.

Having been sorted into public and private, these speeches were coded for timing, location, and content. Every speech was noted for location and date, both the calendar date and the number of days prior to the election. Then, every statement made about any partisan candidate was coded for what was said and the intensity of the statement. Intensity was divided between "appearance" and "endorsement." "Appearance" included any statement by the president about a candidate who was present at the event, including innocuous remarks like "Thanks for coming"; thus, it was the base code for all statements. For something to be coded as an "endorsement," it had to include stronger language signifying a request by the president for those in the audience to aid that individual. Ultimately, it was limited to statements that included the following phrase: "I/[X place] need(s); (re)elect; vote for; send to; make a great; I am/will be for him/her; right man/woman; is essential; speak up for; is good for; needs your help; I look forward to seeing."

These coding guidelines were developed organically from examination of the text, because different presidents used very different language in addressing candidates. The original plan was to use only phrases like "endorse," "support," "elect," or other predetermined phrases. However, on examination, presidents were internally consistent in their own use of phrasing that clearly implied the same level of support, the same request of the public, but in a fashion that was idiosyncratic in regard to other presidents. Early presidents used "endorse," "support," and so forth, but as time went on and the behavior became more personal, presidents shifted to "I need," "I am for," and other statements of personal purpose. Thus, as the analysis developed, what was included expanded but was kept as tight as possible and focused on words with implicit equivalent purpose.

After all the statements were coded, they were tabulated for each candidate. Statements that were coded as "appearance" for private events were not included in the tabulations. These were excluded because they were deemed to be insufficiently important within their setting. "Appearance" statements in public events were included because they invariably included presidential presence with a candidate that could be understood by the crowd (and the media). At a minimum, then, these occasions should have allowed for a photo op. Such statements in private settings, however, would simply have been "hellos" said among other elites; thus, they would be perceived as much less valuable to the candidate. Total days, total events, and total fundraisers were tabulated in addition to tabulating appearances and endorsements, thus allowing each candidate to be broken into four levels of campaigning (none, visited, endorsed, fundraised), as well as to be compared in terms of frequency and style.

Notes

1. No president made full use of a given year, with only two presidents even campaigning in January. See Table 5.3.

2. See, for example, "Statement in Support of Republican Candidates" (October 31, 1970), pp. 1032–33. *Public Papers of the Presidents of the United States: Richard Nixon, 1970.* Nixon was the only president to regularly release written campaign statements during the midterm year; he would release a press statement prior to each set of campaign events to highlight whom he was campaigning for and why.

Ranney Index

At the heart of the examination of the origins of midterm campaigning in Chapter 4 was the examination of party competition at the state level, using a modified Ranney Index. The Ranney Index was first proposed by Austin Ranney in 1965 and served to measure the level of state-level party control. It did this by averaging (1) the proportion of seats in the lower chamber of the legislature held by the Democratic party; (2) the proportion in the upper chamber; (3) the Democratic share of the two-party gubernatorial vote; and (4) the proportion of terms of office for the governor and each chamber for which the Democratic party held control. As such, it allows scholars an index measure of party control over time, capturing the changing party dominance in given states.

The weakness of this measure is that it only captures the level of control—not the level of competitiveness. This is where the folded Ranney Index comes into play. As noted in Chapter 4, this measure, put forward by Gary King in 1989, modifies the Ranney Index by "folding" it over, therefore creating a measure of competition between the parties rather than a measure of control by a single party. The actual "formula" is "[Folded Ranney Index] = 1—[RI–0.5], where IPC is the interparty competition index and RI is the original Ranney Index."[1] Effectively, this argues that a high score on a Ranney Index suggests low levels of competition, and that low scores indicate high levels of competitiveness—and then it simply re-indexes the data by centering them between 0.5 (low) and 1 (high). The advantage to this is obvious, as it makes it much easier to examine how state-level politics has changed rather than merely examining who happens to be in charge at a given moment (a far less interesting question for these purposes).

The reason the (folded) Ranney index was chosen to represent interparty competition is that it does the best job of approximating what this project was looking to examine. There are plenty of alternate measures of party strength that could have been used, each offering different advantages. For example,

Ceaser and Saldin (2005) use a measure that captures a hybrid of both state and national electoral strength, whereas Holbrook and Van Dunk (1993) look specifically at the "pressure" felt by elected officials.[2] However, none of the existing measures do a better job of capturing what is at the heart of the folded Ranney Index—interparty competition at the state level, separate of national factors.[3] Given that the reason for using a measure of party competitiveness is to capture changes in the state-level political climate that might attract or repel presidential activity (separate from national trends).

To bring this into being, and as part of a personal quest to recreate every possible wheel, the data for the Ranney Index used herein were put together by hand, eschewing the use of existing versions. Consequently, any errors that exist are there through my own fault; the finalized Ranney Index is recoverable at MichaelJulius.net. The source data were drawn from the *Book of the States* (legislative share) and the CQ Election Database (governor vote shares). They are meant to accurately replicate any other Ranney Index, apart from looking at *years* of party control rather than terms. The rationale for this was born from the simple fact that (1) state term lengths vary for given offices (therefore rendering interstate comparisons more difficult), and (2) state elections do not necessarily align with each other or with federal elections (see New Jersey and Virginia).

Notes

1. James D. King, "Interparty Competition in the American States: An Examination of Index Components," *The Western Political Quarterly* 42, no. 1 (1989): 85.

2. James W. Ceaser and Robert P. Saldin, "A New Measure of Party Strength," *Political Research Quarterly* 58, no. 2 (2005): 245–56; Timothy M. Holbrook and Emily Van Dunk, "Electoral Competition in the American States," *American Political Science Review* 87, no. 4 (1993): 955–62. Ceaser and Saldin also have a fruitful discussion on the merits of various measures of party competition (before suggesting their own). It is worthwhile reading in order to understand the benefits and costs of each.

3. This is not to discount the salient point raised by Brown and Bruce (2002) that a weakness of the Ranney Index is its focus on outcomes rather than inputs—specifically, that the focus on wins and losses while ignoring the relative closeness of a given race. It does not escape my attention that this is similar to the complaints made above concerning prior examinations of midterm campaign results.

Index

Note: Page numbers followed by *t* indicate tables and *f* indicate figures.

About the Author

Michael A. Julius, PhD, is a lecturer in the Department of Politics at Coastal Carolina University, Conway, SC.